UP TO OUR STEEPLES IN POLITICS

Up to Our Steeples in Politics

by
Will D. Campbell
and
James Y. Holloway

Wipf & Stock
PUBLISHERS
Eugene, Oregon

Wipf and Stock Publishers
199 W 8th Ave, Suite 3
Eugene, OR 97401

Up To Our Steeples in Politics
By Campbell, Will D. and Holloway, James Y.
Copyright©1970 by Campbell, Will D.
ISBN: 1-59244-908-5
Publication date 9/30/2004
Previously published by Paulist Press, 1970

Contents

Foreword		1
I	Katallagete!	7
II	Law and Love	21
III	Deceptive Words	31
IV	Footwashing or the New Hermeneutic?	39
V	Milestones into Millstones	51
VI	Politics as Baal	59
VII	The Paradigm of Dixie Hills	75
VIII	If We Should Get Serious	87
IX	Violence and Snopes	91
X	A Homily on Patriotism	103
XI	Up to Our Steeples in Politics	111
XII	Our Grade Is "F"	129
XIII	What Are We Going To Do Now?	151

*To our parents
who taught us to read the Bible*

Foreword

In one of his letters to the Christians in Corinth, St. Paul uses the imperative, *katallagete:* "In Christ's name, we implore you, be reconciled *(katallagete)* to God!" (2 Cor. 5, 20). This word, directed to Christians and to the Christian communities, is of interest to "the world" only if the world finds it interesting, or if God should, in his own purposes, decide to interest the world in it. This book is primarily an effort to understand the implications of Paul's imperative, *katallagete,* for Christians at the end of the 20th century.

We agree with those who have reminded us in recent years that the Christian faith is *indicative* (the *fact* that God reconciles the world in Christ), not *imperative (Go* to church! *Do* not drink bourbon! *Feed* the hungry! *Search* and *destroy!).* But we believe that St. Paul's imperative use of "reconcile" calls attention to a special kind of behavior by the Christian toward the world, behavior which "does" by *being,* "acts" by *living—* that is, *being* and *living* as God made us in Christ.

This book is a series of statements about our understanding of *why* St. Paul uses the imperative form of "to reconcile" and how that "why" speaks clearly and unmistakably to what the world defines today as social issues and political problems. It is, for that reason, a discussion of our conviction that the Christian communities have failed in their calling, their ministry, because (at their liberal best) they sought to do for the world what God *has already done* for the world in Christ: the work of reconciliation.

This book talks about our conviction that "already the axe is laid to the root of the trees" (Lk. 3, 9) *because* the Church is trying to share shirts and food with the poor and the hungry as imperative programs of social action, programs the Church apparently believes are required by a law of God. We are trying to argue in these pages that St. Paul's imperative—Be reconciled to God!—means that God wants *not* doing, but *being; not* social action, but *living; not* welfare, but *witness.* Sharing? Yes! *Not* as a program, but as a parable, a thanksgiving, for what God has done for us in Christ!

In our day, we in the Church have tried to do God's job, while at the same time rejecting the *only* job God puts before us. We have tried to reconcile people and groups of people by using every gimmick and technique that culture uses to sell its automobiles, deodorants, civil repression and international warfare. We have tried surveys, group dynamics, T-groups, political activism, sociological and psychological processing, and all the well-known foolishness of church socials, retreats, picnics, bowling alleys, swimming pools, skating rinks, gymnasiums, counseling centers, marriage-and-the-family instruction, relevant ministries and updated theological schools—all pleasant, on occasion even controversial, but having nothing, *absolutely nothing,* to do with the mission of Christians as ambassadors of, witnesses to, what God has done for all men in Christ.

But we in the Church persist: we are still hopeful that through all those means we can build a kingdom in which all things will be set right between man and man (and occasionally between man and God), refusing to recognize that these means are an attempt to build a kingdom by *our* guidelines and blueprints, by *our* sociology and politics, not by what God's reconciliation has already done for the world in Christ. In this book we are trying to confess that the goals of the contemporary Church—that is to say, the church of St. John's by the Gas Station, the Christian college, the denominational and interdenominational seminary—the *goals* of these Christian communities are blasphemous. The reconciliation the Church is seeking to accomplish today by these subterfuges has already been wrought. The brotherhood—the "one blood" of Acts 17, 26—that the Church makes its goal today is already a *fact.* And because this is so, that very fact judges our goals and our efforts to achieve brotherhood by social action as blasphemous, as trying to *be* God. Instead of witnessing to Christ, the social action of the Church lends support to the totalitarianism of wars and political systems of the 20th century. By its social action, the Church permits and encourages the State and culture to define all issues and rules and fields of battle. The Church then tries to do what the State, without the Church's support, had already decided to do: to "solve" *all* human problems by politics. And this is specifically the political messianism of contemporary totalitarianism and of Revelation 13. "Politics" by definition can only "adjust" and "rearrange." It cannot—as politics—"solve" anything. But the Church's social action encourages the very movements in the contemporary political processes which are moving us straightaway into 20th-century totalitarianism.

The Church has, in a word, tried to effect reconciliation where there already *is* reconciliation, while the *only* thing that God ever asked from the Church was to *live* thanksgiving for others and so express thanksgiving for what he has done for us! Thus we talk in these pages about the Christian community in apostasy, for we believe that when the Christian community tries to *do* what God has already done, it is living a lie.

That is why we have failed as Christians. And failure to recognize the failure compounds our apostasy. St. Paul's imperative, "Be reconciled *(katallagete)* to God," inasmuch as we *are* reconciled to God, has no advice about what "to do." It has much to say about what "to be." We must *be* what we are—what we *already* are by God's doing, not ours. And what *are* we already? We are in Christ, reconciled to God and therefore to man. We believe that St. Paul's imperative leaves no room for what the Church calls "social action." To engage in what the Church calls "social action" is purely and simply to lie about reconciliation, to live as if it were obedience to law, to try to please God (and ourselves) by what *we* do by and for ourselves, and so reject the gift of what he did for us in Christ. Yet St. Paul's imperative—"Be reconciled to God"—is the only social action there is for the Christian: life as a thanksgiving to God. Such a life involves the giving of food to the hungry, drink to the thirsty, shelter to the homeless and clothes to the naked—in other words, life as the Good News, life as thanksgiving for what God did for us. Not social action, for this rejects the gift of grace and contradicts the Good News by turning it into the Bad News of programs, strategies, imperatives, laws and acts of obedience which, in trying to "please" God and ourselves with what *we* do for him, in fact recrucifies him.

In this book, we talk about racism, politics, war, poverty, education, and the coming of America's technological police state. But in no sense is this a handbook of social action or strategy suggestions for the Christian in politics. This is merely our effort to understand a fact—a fact, it must be emphasized, with which we had nothing to do. It is our discussion of the fact of *God's* reconciliation of all men as it bears on the racism, politics, war, poverty, education and police states that characterize the 20th century.

But what about enmity, estrangement, alienation—realities which loom so large in the writings of St. Paul, despite his use of other (and probably more effective) words and descriptions? What of prejudice and the brokenness of the human family? How can we presume to say that man is *already* reconciled in Christ when all about us is the living hell of alienation, enmity and estrangement? We are not in these pages talking about being "reconciled" to racism's inhumanity, war's idolatry and death, education's totalitarianism or politics' messianism. We are saying that these blasphemies so characteristic of our age can be understood by the Christian and are judged by God *only* in the light of his reconciliation of all men in Christ. We are trying to talk in these pages about *God's* reconciliation of *us,* and not about our efforts to reconcile ourselves, efforts that have brought about the very enmities, estrangements and alienations that characterize the 20th century. We are talking about Thomas Merton's conviction that "to reconcile man with man and not with God is to reconcile no one at all."

We are reconciled to God, whether we know it or not, whether we want it or not. But this reconciliation is God's way of doing, not ours. It came to us as a gift, not as reward or law. As a gift, it is meant for us to accept. However, it can also—because it is a gift—be rejected, turned back, cursed, denied, and bring forth the fruits of enmities, estrangements and alienations and the blasphemies of social action. But because God did it, not man, because it is a gift and not a commandment, because it is life, not law, our blasphemies are not and cannot be the last word. The *only* Word is life, not death, resurrection, not annihilation. This is the *fact*. All the rest are the ideals of the social action which deny the Good News of what God did for us in Christ. And this means quite simply, in St. Paul's words, that "worldly standards"—beauty, sex, ugliness, money, race, poverty, complexion, politics, nationality, education, lack of education, shape, size, culture, culture-deprivation—these and any other such standards no longer hold power over the way we act toward God or toward others. We no longer need to behave as if "the world" or even we ourselves were making judgments on ourselves or on the world, or engage in the festivals which please the world or ourselves. Worldly standards no longer control the way we behave; they cannot alter this new and fundamental relationship which now exists between God and man, and between man and man, because of what *God* did by reconciling us to himself, beginning the "new creation" of men reconciled to each other in Christ. To proclaim—which is to say, to live—this News is the "service of reconciliation" of which St. Paul speaks, and this is the *only* thing God ever "asks." Not social action, not human engineering, not gimmicks or techniques that try to bring men together with other men—these deny that the News of Christ is Good, since they affirm that he lived and died in vain and did not rise again for our salvation. God "asks" *only* that we live the whole of our lives so that it corresponds to, is a witness of, proclaims the truth about, what God has done for us all in Christ. Anything else for the Christian is to live a lie, because it lives as if the Event of Christ is of no account.

Do? Nothing! Be? What you *are:* a weak, helpless child whom God loves as Christ loves and has brought together (reconciled) in the Event, which is the imperative (*katallagete*) to live the truth of Christ—with no questions asked!—regardless of who we are and what we have done! That "service" is the imperative, *katallagete,* of the indicative, reconciliation.

That service is what these pages seek to discuss. Whether that notion is reactionary or radical, liberal or conservative, is of no concern to us. These terms are irrelevant to the biblical notions we are trying to uncover.

Many of these essays appeared in somewhat different form in the journal of the Committee of Southern Churchmen which bears the name of St. Paul's imperative: *Katallagete*—Be reconciled. The Committee, of which we are a part, has always been concerned with most of the issues we talk about in these pages. Of course, not all those who belong to the Committee would agree with what we are saying. But they know, as we know, that this is not what is important.

So whether or not you read further, whether you agree or disagree, we bid you, in God's name: *Katallagete!*

I
Katallagete!

His purpose in dying for all was that men, while still in life, should cease to live for themselves, and should live for him who for their sake died and was raised to life. With us therefore worldly standards have ceased to count in our estimate of any man; even if once they counted in our understanding of Christ, they do so now no longer. When anyone is united to Christ, there is a new world; the old order has gone, and a new order has already begun.

From first to last this has been the work of God. He has reconciled us men to himself through Christ, and he has enlisted us in this service of reconciliation. What I mean is that God was in Christ reconciling the world to himself, no longer holding men's misdeeds against them, and that he has entrusted us with the message of reconciliation.

(2 Corinthians 5, 15-20)

We have been calling it "social action" when all the while it was evangelism.

That word falls as judgment on the life and faith of the communities of Christians at the end of the 20th century. The New Testament finds us in apostasy. St. Paul says that Christ died "for all," so "that men, while still in life, should cease to live for themselves, and should live for him who for their sake died and was raised to life. With us therefore worldly standards have ceased to count in our estimate of any man." Yet our actions in the 20th century on the "problem" of race deny our confession that Christ is Lord because, segregationists and integrationists alike, we have made "race" a category, a "worldly standard." We have accepted without a murmur of complaint racists' phrases of "segregation" and "integration"—phrases which have absolutely no meaning in or for the Church. The Church is the *body of Christ,* and the Gospel the *Good News* about what God did and does for man, despite what man did and does to God.

Paul says that the Good News "from first to last . . . has been the work of God." But we have denied both the efficacy and the relevance of this work of God for all men by tying *his* work to the work of *our* hands. As the folk-church in the South, we have denied Christ's purpose of "dying for all" in the apostasy that the body of Christ is either all-white or all-black or black-and-white. As a national Church we have denied Paul's insistent reminder that the "new order" which the Church proclaims by *its words and deeds* has been "from first to last . . . the work of God." We have made civil rights and integration the end, the goal, the *telos* for Christian witness, thus tying the work of the Church to the decisions of political authorities and social scientists, decisions that to all but the blind or willful or frightened are clearly indecisive, insufficient and idolatrous.

So we have turned our back on proclaiming in word but particularly in deeds the *only* message that the Church—the body of Christ—has ever had for "the world" and its activities: "In Christ's name, we implore you, be reconciled *(katallagete)* to God!"

We believe, therefore, that Paul's affirmations about the work of the Church can clarify our faith and our work in the South, in this nation, and in the world, in the 1970's. Unquestionably, the use of Scripture in this way, to clarify the faith and the life of men enmeshed in the 20th century, has something to do with the problem of the authority of Scripture. But let us also remember that the problem of Scripture's authority is also concerned with the authority of the ideas and the ideologies and the priorities peculiar to the world at the end of the 20th century. The South is often called the "Bible Belt," directing attention to our distinctive manner of exploiting the Bible and the Christian faith as a sanction for the dehumanizing relationship that exists between the peoples of the South. Yet, a large part of the Western world takes pride in having—or deludes itself into thinking that it has—"come of age," signifying in this connection another, although related, sort of exploitation of the Bible. This latter stems from the conviction that any statement from the infantile world of the Bible must be filtered through the achievement and wisdom of the mature world of the 20th century.

The truth is, Scripture has no more in common with the latter endeavor than it does with the former, for the simple reason that both make use of the Bible in a thoroughly unbiblical manner. While the men of the Bible Belt (and their sophisticated allies elsewhere) are unwilling to acknowledge the fact that Scripture is a book in history about what happens to men in history when God becomes flesh "to dwell among us . . . full of grace and truth," the men (and especially their allies in churches) who glory in and celebrate their modernity are unwilling to acknowledge the relative, historical quality of the ideas about faith and life which the 20th century shares with the 16th or 1st centuries, A.D. or B.C.

In taking Paul's letters as an authoritative point of departure, we mean no more than Karl Barth meant forty years ago when he explained that his "biblicism" consisted in nothing more than being "prejudiced in supposing the Bible to be a good book," and "profitable for men to take its conceptions at least as seriously as they take their own." But if our use of Paul's understanding of Christian communities means no more than that, it means *at least that*. It means, for example, that the authoritative character and quality of God's ways and Way with man recorded in Scripture are denied when Scripture is employed as a repository of ideals and principles to justify the strategies of the social obscurantist or social revolutionary. Scripture concerns man's ways with man in the light of God's ways and Way with man; it is concerned with man's ideals about himself and his fellows only as they might affirm or contradict God's ways and Way with men. For this, if for no other reason, the message of the Bible cannot be employed as a political expedient.

Paul's letters are imposed upon us irrevocably and inescapably because their message of the purpose and consequences of Christ's dying and being "raised to life" *for all men* speaks directly to the broken relationships between and among men in the South and in the world in our time. Indeed, this message of God's work of reconciliation through Christ is the only way in which the blasphemies, violences, deaths and deceits of our time are finally comprehensible: through faith in "his purpose in dying for all."

Paul's letter to the Christians in Corinth, for example, makes it clear that our distinguishing failure—or, to put the matter more accurately, our chief sin—as a Church is theological, not sociological or functional, and that, for those individuals (and those institutions peculiar to individuals) who confess Christ as Lord, the consequence is a call for repentance and a prayer for renewal, not strategic reevaluation or functional reorganization. By "theological" we mean simply to call attention to the primacy of *God's* determination of our relationships with all men. *God's* reconciliation of "us men to himself through Christ" requires that our faith and our lives reflect in obedience the *fact* of this reconciliation. Not only is this requirement other—and, we believe, more serious and more radical—than demands for political rights and social integration, but it also directs and determines our work in and for political rights and social integration. We believe that Paul's admonition describes our task as "churchmen" to be ambassadors of Christ's reconciliation of all men—and that this very description judges our current failure as churchmen in the South to be basically theological, rather than being sociologically or functionally irrelevant to what is going on in the movements for social and racial integration and political rights.

Of[8] course, the sins of the Church are always fundamentally theological; other failures should be of interest to us, but they should not absorb or entice us away from our principal trust.

Whenever they do, we invariably are hankering after the approval of the powerful and wise of the world. The service to which Christians have been entrusted is the message—that is, the "Good News"—that "he has reconciled us men to himself through Christ," the fruits of which were and are not postponed for a life to come (this would be only moderately "good news"), and that *now,* "while still in life," men are able to "cease to live for themselves" because Christ has already lived and died *for* and *in* us. That event and that event alone explains how the Christian ought to act in the world out of the conviction that "worldly standards have ceased to count."

This is the "theology"—the "Good News"—we reject when we proclaim ourselves, our race, our politics, our churches. Other failures—especially our temporizing about racism and political rights—were strategic, and it is far, far too late now to undo them. Yet these strategic failures stem directly and inevitably from the theological failure. The sin of the churches is exemplified in our persistent, determined, frantic, and generally massive efforts to reject the service of reconciliation—which is to say, the service of evangelism—as Paul described it to the Christians in Corinth. As an organization, institution and bureaucracy in American life, the Church has been moderately successful, considering its overall lack of social sophistication on the one hand, and the internal quibblings between bureaucrats and professors, laity and ministers, on the other. But this success, or moderate success, is both irrelevant to and a contradiction of the work and service which distinguish the Church as the body of Christ.

The Church has failed to "evangelize." This is precisely what we mean by a theological and not a sociological failure: the failure to live the "Good News" in the world of politics—the world in which Christ lived—and the failure thereby to reject the "revivalism" by which, twice a year, we have merely congratulated and perpetuated our own kind politically, socially, and racially. "Evangelism" begins when the Christian lives the confession of "Good News": "He has reconciled us men to himself through Christ. . . . With us *therefore* worldly standards have ceased to count in our estimate of any man." The "worldly standards" of race and class are most obvious, but there are other devices—politics, economics, education, geography, dialect, sex, nationality, and, above all, religion—by which we have sought to justify ourselves from the power of meaninglessness and the judgment of sin and death. Kierkegaard's various attacks on "the monstrous illusion of Christendom" have more to say to us about the Church and evangelism in the 1970's than denominational (and certainly non-denominational) journals, ecumenical statements, or seminars and study groups on the "nature" of the Church.

"It is as if God were appealing to you *through us*" is a word of judgment, because what has been appealed to the world "*through us*" as churchmen in the past two decades cannot stand too long the light of day, and will not stand at all in the Light of life. But this same word may also be the word of renewal, for the Church becomes the body of Christ in and through its proclamation by deed and by word in service to "the message of reconciliation." Whatever else the Church "is" to social scientists and strategists, to Christians the Church "is" its work, and this "work" is to be with men, not movements; with people, not principles or ideals; with the men of the world regardless of and despite their movements and principles and ideals—no questions asked!—simply because this is the way Christ was and is with the men of the world. This is the work of churchmen that Paul describes in speaking about "Christ's ambassadors": "It is as if God were appealing to you through us: In Christ's name, we implore you, be reconciled to God."

Katallagete! "Be reconciled," since we are all already reconciled in Christ's "purpose in dying for all." This is the only word the Christian brings to the broken relationships between and among men. Because the source of reconciliation, the Word made flesh, "came to dwell among us," we have no doubt about where the service of reconciliation ought to lead: not into the falsely secure world of a Christendom which denies the work of the Lord by its defensiveness and isolation, but into the genuinely insecure world of politics, wars, poverty, hunger, violence and insurrection—that is, the world into which Christ came and lived, by which he was murdered, and for which he died and was raised to life.

Of course, there is a sense in which it is absurd to insist that "Be reconciled *(katallagete)* to God" is the *only* word that is peculiar to the Church's life for the world. That is the sense which will occur to those who see the Civil Rights Acts of 1964 and 1965, the Supreme Court decisions and similar "gains" as the solution to America's race problem. Those who see the role a few church groups played in influencing these happenings as being the faithful mission and witness of the Church will also find it strange and absurd to use Scripture as the guideline, the plumb line, for the activity of Church and churchmen.

The truth is, as we see it, that insofar as America's race problem is concerned, we churchmen, as "ambassadors" of "the message of reconciliation," have not solved the race problem. Indeed, we doubt that the problem has even been discovered, because we continue to be embarrassed that being an "ambassador" of reconciliation means evangelism, not "social action."

We also find that there is a strange confusion about whose problem is "what." Society assumed that its problem was race. Now it is coming to understand that its problem was not so much race but poverty. As for the Church, when it bothered to see social ills at all, it concerned itself with almsgiving and relieving the suffering of the poor. Now it appears to believe that if it is ever to see itself as that body described by Paul in which "worldly standards have ceased to count," in which all have already been made brothers and sisters in a more binding way than blood birth, the prior problem the Church must settle is one of "race." And that is just the point. For *that* solution must go beyond race to a Christian doctrine of man in which race is abolished.

During the past few years a segment of the Church has sought to settle the "question" of race. But the problem was seen as discrimination between races, not the abolition of the very concept of race in the life of the Church. Even in dealing with prejudice and discrimination, we, at our best, merely indicated that we were willing to enter the arena of social reform, and at much the same level as other institutions of society.

Although the changes which have been wrought in race relations are sometimes referred to as a revolution, there was never more than social reform involved, for what the civil rights leaders of the past insisted upon was simply that America be faithful to the political document—the Constitution—which brought it into being. There was no suggestion that it be amended, or that our social system be altered.

Today there is every indication that more than social reform is in the offing. Drastic and far-reaching changes are being called for. One does not have to go to the followers of the late Malcolm X to see that what is being demanded now are radical and immediate changes in the American system in order for a more equitable distribution of the nation's wealth to become a reality. That is a far, far different thing than calling for first-come first-seated on a bus, the right to a cup of coffee if you have a dime, or the right to register and vote if you have finished the sixth grade. Talk to former members of the Student Nonviolent Coordinating Committee or even the predominately white Students for a Democratic Society or Southern Student Organizing Committee, to say nothing of Weathermen. They are not talking in terms of mild social reform. Nor do they see the American political system as anything sacred. If the goals they seek can be reached within the present system, that is all right. If they cannot, they are for amending the system at least or wrecking the old one as a start.

There is little evidence that any segment of the Church in America is any more prepared to speak to this development than it was prepared a decade ago (or two years ago) to speak to the mild social reform movement concerned chiefly with civil rights.

During the first year or so of the 1960's the more radical (or "enlightened") elements within the churches said that they were then willing to enter the arena of social reform. This was done largely through the National Council of Churches Commission on Religion and Race, plus a few denominational groups such as the United Presbyterian Commission on Religion and Race, the National Council of the Episcopal Church's Division of Christian Citizenship and the United Church of Christ's Racial Justice Now. There is little to indicate that even these agencies and their personnel have thought out a position if true revolution should become a fact. On the contrary, there is growing evidence that some of these groups used their power and influence to "freeze out" the political revolutionaries. This is not to suggest that such action is either right or wrong. It is to suggest that if, a few years ago, the activist segment of the Protestant Establishment thought that participation in the mild social reform movement would place Protestantism on the "right side" in the eyes of black masses grown tired of our new moons and solemn assemblies, they were mistaken, pathetically so. On the other hand, if this participation in civil rights reform represented genuine repentance and the intention to lead a new life, the opportunity to lead that new life is now at hand.

But the point here is to plead that the Church Establishment not make the mistake it did early in the past decade prior to its entry into the social reform movement. At that time, the Church on the whole, and at its best, remained in a state of hypnotic indecision until the phase of social reform was near completion. The action it finally took was in an atmosphere where its guilt made it impossible to be anything but desperate and sentimental, and with not enough status to be either objective or critical. For the most part the best they could do was to follow some of the more militant groups who appeared to be going *somewhere*. Apparently, it did not occur to the Church to ask itself exactly *where* it was going so long as it went. And such following as it did was often more like a playful father appearing to follow his child into deep water to assure him of his presence, knowing that when the danger point was reached he could resume the leadership and save them both.

The water has turned out to be not the mild sea of racial desegregation but the raging surf of political redirection. The cutting edge of the movement now is not concerned with filling the stools of lunch counters, but with organizing the poor so that they set the policy, produce the leadership, run the show, cease to be the poor—be they black or white. It is a tempest to which the playful father cannot now say "Peace, be still," and expect to walk happily together back to the secure shores of the past.

During the Johnson-Goldwater campaign white "backlash" did not develop because at that time the majority of "haves" could see nothing in the demands of the minority of "have-nots" to cause them to have less. "Let them, in the name of economic growth, eat at Morrison's Cafeteria. I eat at the Club anyway." The backlash became a reality because the established "haves" now realize that they are being called upon to have less, so that the "have-nots" may have more. To shrug this off with moans of "communism!" is to miss the whole point. To suggest that America's revolutionaries of the left are directed from Moscow or Peking is like saying that the John Birch Society is directed from Portugal or the White Citizens Council from South Africa.

Exactly what form this movement will take is not clear to anyone, including those who would lead it. What *is* clear is that white America, at its best, saw as its day of reckoning the Supreme Court decision of 1954 and the Civil Rights Acts of 1964 and 1965. But that was not its day of reckoning at all. It was but the first morning stirring of the cock to suggest that the day is approaching. The reason that Supreme Court decisions and civil rights legislation were not its day of reckoning is very simple. They came too late.

As proud as we may be of what some churchmen have done during the past decade, we know that even this, belated and little as it was, did not represent the thinking of the majority of churchgoers.

If this represented our best efforts to obey the prophets' call for social justice, what will we be able to produce in revolution, particularly a revolution which stands no more chance of success than the Hungarian or Czechoslovakian revolt, but which would require even more drastic means to put down?

The alternative would seem to be that the Church either once again serve as chaplain to the status quo—"too bad about the methods but *they* did get violent, you know"—or else equate the revolution with the kingdom of God and join it uncritically and with abandon. Much of the "white church" is apt to do the first. Some of the "black church" is apt to do the latter. And if we are confronted with one or the other as the Church's grand strategy, where does it lead us except to where we are now? Is either the mission of the Church? If the status quo had more to be said for it, or if the consummation of past revolutions had a better record, the answer might be simpler. (And we must be careful now, lest we say "a plague on both your heads" and thereby side, in pious neutrality, with the stronger.) If there is a mission for us, it is one which God has provided and not we ourselves.

In a region where it is simply assumed that everyone is a churchman, particularly if he is in public office, we hesitate to say that anyone is not a Christian or that his conduct is not Christian. George Wallace was a delegate to his Methodist Conference and Ross Barnett is faithful in attendance and leadership at his Baptist Sunday School. We feel it an embarrassing presumption to go to such a man with the bold proclamation: "Repent, George Wallace, and believe the Gospel!" His response is apt to be, "Do you know something I do not know? Have you been singled out so that God has revealed something to you he has not revealed to me and others?" To such a response we can only reply, "That is quite possible." For it would seem that such a man does not have the same commitment as those who see the kingdom of Christ as one in which worldly standards such as race have ceased to count, in which we are already reconciled, where the old order, glorious as it might have been, is gone and a new order has already begun.

Yes, we know something they do not know. We know that God so loved *the world,* with *all* its people, their sins and problems, that he became like one of us and dwelt among us and died that we might all be one people—his people. We know that God was in Christ, reconciling the world to himself and breaking down all barriers and walls of hostility which separate us from one another and from him. We know that God, in establishing the Church, has enlisted us to proclaim that message of reconciliation. We know that we are called not to build a kingdom, but to bid men to enter one already established, here and now, in which race is as irrelevant a category as redhead, baldhead, fat man, lean man. We also know that Jesus fed the hungry and healed the sick and bade his followers do the same.

That is what we know, and that is the evangelical message we must now proclaim to both revolutionary and defender of the status quo. And to those who would say we have not earned the right to preach to the revolutionaries, we can only say, "God, in Christ, has earned it for us."

The Church has failed in the matter of race because we have called it "social action" when all the while it was evangelism.

Whether this evangelism can be wrought within the present structure of the Church remains to be seen. Certainly the pietist influence which has dominated Southern revivalism for two centuries and succeeded so well in keeping the Church *out of* the world cannot be its strength. The social gospel which did go into the world but took so little of the Church with it cannot be its present help. It must instead be based on a well-defined orthodoxy. And it must be an orthodoxy which takes it into the streets, not as a gimmick to take us where the most people are (though this is true), but because here is the lump to be leavened, the "those for whom Christ died," a Christ who lived in the streets and died at its hands.

And somebody, sometime, will provide everything else—the President, the Congress, the Court, effective civil rights organizations.

But it cannot be an evangelism of revivalistic recruitment of large numbers. No region has ever been more guilty of such cheap and vulgar dodges of true evangelism than our Southland.

Katallagete! 19

The bigger barns we have built line the highways and adorn the cities. That it has not resulted in a redeemed community which serves as the leavening of society must now be obvious to all who have even glanced at the dry bones of Southern folk religion. There is little doubt but that those who beat, killed and buried the three civil rights workers in Neshoba County did so in the name of Jesus Christ. Because this is the case, many would abandon evangelism. But how can something be abandoned which has not really been tried? No one, not even Madison Avenue, has been more successful in recruitment than the churches of the South. And no one has failed more miserably at evangelism.

Repeatedly those of us who attend conferences on social action hear it lamented that the Church has "lost its mission." The speaker generally infers that the *mission* of the Church is "social action." He does not seem to realize that his own Division of Social Action was probably created by the Establishment to avoid evangelism and thus to avoid the heart of social action for the churches—an evangelism that sees all of life as incarnational, a social action that follows as naturally as breathing.

And can the Church really lose its mission? Only if and when it assumes that it created the mission. God constantly provides the mission to go over to Nineveh and proclaim the Word of the Lord. We saw Nineveh as the race problem, but like Jonah we keep catching the wrong boat to get there and find ourselves in the whale's belly of legalistic reform.

The one boat we haven't boarded to reach this Nineveh is evangelism. It is doubtful that the Church will ever do anything significant until we in the Church board the ark of evangelism.

For somebody, sometime, will provide everything else.

Katallagete!

II
Law and Love

If one thing is clear in the New Testament it is the central theme of the triumph of grace over law. While Paul stopped short of a rigid antinomian position, a complete disregard for law, he did make it clear that to abide *in* grace is more radical than to abide *by* law. And such law as he did emphasize was not law in the sense of the entreaties by the State to make us behave, but an ethics, the fruit of the Spirit, resulting from being "in Christ." Far more radical than law was the acceptance of this freedom.

Unless and until Christians who remain in the civil rights movement go to the white segregationist with that radical word, we will continue to be little more than a pitiful, irrelevant addendum to the humanistically oriented organizations which got along quite well without us during our long period of silence and inactivity.

The real issue now is the *failure of law* in the racial crisis. (If anyone sees a few recent "convictions" in the South as a denial of this, let him understand that "failure of law" does not have to do with conviction or acquittal but with the fact that the acts were committed in the first place.) So to go on crying, "More law!" or "Better law!" or even "Federal law!" is to beg the question. It is akin to using aspirin for a headache long after it is discovered that the headache is caused by a brain tumor. There is no question that aspirin is a remarkable drug and continues to have its place even in the presence of a brain tumor. But to rush around to find better aspirin—aspirin with bufferin, aspirin that will dissolve minutes faster, aspirin with a combination of ingredients—simply because that is all the pharmacist could provide, is to place too much confidence in the pharmacist and too little in his allies of medical science. The patient is dying. We are suspicious of surgery for brain tumor because a few practitioners have grafted the reproductive organs of goats onto human beings with the claim that it would restore one to youthful vitality.

The Christian doctrine of grace is suspect in the racial crisis because "the South has had that preached to it for two hundred years and it hasn't done any good." The only trouble with that claim is that it simply is not true. The folk religion of the South has been a religion of law, not of grace, and it continues to be such. As Harry Caudill observed in *Night Comes to the Cumberlands* concerning the Appalachian South, the South has never been the Bible Belt in the sense of a depth of understanding of the Bible. He points out that many rural folk of that area did not even have Bibles, and if they had them, they seldom could read them.

The religion that developed in the South was a strange combination of Indian lore, old wives' tales, bits of Stoic doctrine passed on by the educated aristocracy, and superstitions based on biblical quotations remembered from the time the Methodist or Baptist itinerant preacher spent the night on his way to Natchez or Atlanta.

The religious problem of the South is not biblical literalism but biblical illiteracy.

When this religion did move the South, it was generally in the form of a rigid legalism, and, for much the same reason, legalism is what we are promoting today with the civil rights legislation. To solve a problem you get people to believe certain things, by law. The drunkenness, knife fighting and general unruliness of the frontier South was not conducive to the success of mine, mill and field. What better way to control that than to proclaim that the devil will get you if you don't watch out? Thou shalt not fight, thou shalt not get drunk or cause others to get drunk through the making and selling of "the stuff," and, above all, thou shalt not come to work late on Monday or run away if you are a slave. That is not biblical literalism, and it is certainly not New Testament literalism unless one wants to twist Paul's letter to Philemon into a letter to Onesimus.

And this legalism failed. The South has the finest laws but without a corresponding relationship to its crime rate. (It is true that the F.B.I. recently rated Mississippi as having the second lowest crime rate in the nation—next to Alaska—but if one considers the seventeen men accused of murdering three civil rights workers and remembers that so far none of them have been either indicted or convicted, one can see that the crime rate would be accordingly lowered.)

Legalism is failing again. Whether we can see it now or not, it is failing. It fails because the first lesson man taught himself was how to deal with the requirements of the law. From Eve to Lee Harvey Oswald it has been the same. The way to handle law is to interpret it. Thus "Thou shalt not steal" means "Children should not take apples from other children's lunch baskets"—but it does not have anything to do with price fixing or cheap labor or the stock market. To "Thou shalt not commit adultery" is added "unless your wife doesn't understand you." "Thou shalt not kill" means "One man does not take a gun and shoot a fellow he admits he hates," but it does not apply to a nation killing thousands of men, women and children whom it claims to love.

Yet, if we seem now to advocate the repeal of recently enacted civil rights laws or to oppose the passage of others, we are being less than clear, or are being deliberately misunderstood. We are not suggesting that love and law contradict each other. The point is that those of us who should be interested in relating the two seem not to be relating them at all but to be promoting law and ignoring love, with the further point that the one we insist on promoting continues to fail us.

Law! We must have Federal law to prevent church bombings in the South and to protect minority people against the evil deeds of the majority. Therefore we were given such law. Yet, to our knowledge, not one bombing or dynamiting of a minority-owned business, house of worship or school has been solved by the F.B.I., the agency responsible at the national level. Still, we have law. And the law is used. But it is not used for the reason that brought church folks to march in the streets. The Chase Manhattan Bank and the General Motors and R.C.A. buildings are bombed in New York City. Two days later, four people are arrested and held on half a million dollar bail. The law might have been passed in the name of four Sunday School girls murdered at their prayers in Birmingham. Seven years later, their murderers are free and the dirt slowly collapses around their rotting flesh and pretty little voile shrouds. Those who placed the bombs in the Chase Manhattan Bank and the General Motors and R.C.A. buildings are held on $500,000 bail.

And we have had yet another decision from the Supreme Court on school desegregation. This time, after fifteen years, we are assured that it is the *last* decision. The dual school system must go! *Now! That* is law. And gynecologists report a great upsurge in request for birth control pills in the target states ("They say they don't want to raise any more children to have to go to integrated schools"). And white parents band together to buy a house close to a predominately white school—they have no intention of anyone living there, but the address is what is necessary to keep children in "predominately white schools." The pattern the North developed over a period of a hundred years must now be accomplished quickly in the South. The righteous go on pressing for more law, liberal law. And still more and more blacks say, "We are done with your integration." And more and more of the righteous liberals say: " 'They' don't know what 'they' want."

That is what law is doing for us.

If law is for the purpose of preventing crime, every wail of a siren calls out its failure. Every civil rights demonstration attests to the courts' inability to provide racial justice. Every police chief or F.B.I. director who asks for a larger appropriation because of the rising crime rate is admitting his own failure. Every time a law has to be *enforced* it is a failure.

The simple fact is that, for the Christian, law is an inadequate minimal. Do not even the publicans do the same? If this is all we have to offer the world, then Jesus Christ was of all men the most mad.

Still we hear, "But the racists must be restrained." Exactly! But then where is the fruit? When *will* they be restrained! The truth is that the racists now see a truce being signed between their two traditional enemies, black leaders and the Federal government. No doubt, this has been necessary in moving in the direction of simple justice, especially when such men have declined offers to be a party to the truce. Be that as it may, the rejections continue, the killings go on, the hostilities mount and intensify, perhaps to be set loose wholesale again on another day when the Feds and the Marchers have all gone home, or turned to stopping the war with Venus, and what we see as the gains of *this* day turn out to be the rack rent of *that* day.

The further truth is that such men have not yet been effectively restrained. Law succeeds in putting them in a cage but they continue to shoot through the bars.

If the argument now is on the basis of what will work, then let us put it there.

Few criminologists today see punishment, and especially capital punishment, as an effective deterrent to crime. Recently we have had the frustrating experience of working with a group on a frantic, around-the-clock basis in an effort to abolish capital punishment in a certain state. The argument that got the most votes in the legislature was the finding of leading criminologists. Since that time some of those same individuals have marched in the streets over the acquittal of a murderer. When they hear, "You are after revenge," they reply, "No, not revenge. A preventive." This is sheer madness.

What then do we say? Certainly we cannot say that we are not interested in stopping the killings all around us. Any Christian who is not involved to the maximum in correcting the injustices of the nation and of his own region had best examine his commitment to Christ. Certainly we cannot say we are not interested in the success of the civil rights movement. Too long we debated the number of angels on the head of a pin while our brothers were in chains. Certainly we cannot advocate retreating from the world into the security of established religion. God knows that didn't work! But the question is: What is one's maximum involvement? Is it law, or is there a still deeper issue and involvement?

What distinctive word, what message of hope does the Christian have for the racial crisis? It may be that he has no word of hope in the sense that hope is understood generally. But he certainly has a distinctive word. That word is *The Word—The Word* become flesh.

And that *Word* leads us to the death of Jonathan Daniels in 1965 and our response to it. Jonathan, a student at the Episcopal Theological Seminary in Cambridge, Massachusetts, who was in Alabama for summer civil rights work, was murdered a few moments after his release from a county jail, where he had been incarcerated after participating in a civil rights demonstration.

What can one say when a brother whom we have set apart and sent forth is dead? We can say, "Our brother is dead. Let's go bury him." Then we can say a benediction. And perhaps nothing more is appropriate.

But we churchmen who set Jon Daniels apart and sent him forth said far more than that. We demanded and received immediate appointments with the highest official of the Department of Justice. We pressured through press releases and statements and marches and court stays for Federal intervention. We said such things as: "We must have Federal initiative and involvement in the investigation and prosecution of murders." And then we considered civil proceedings of our own against the murderer of our brother. We indicated that the President is a scoundrel for not "doing something." And worst of all we said that unless the conditions which we set forth were met, Jonathan would have died in vain.

Yes, that last is worst of all, because now nothing, absolutely nothing, any of us do or do not do will cause his death to have been in vain. That is out of our hands. He can never have died in vain because he loved his killer. By his own last written words he loved his killer. According to those words, he did not love him (that is, Alabama) the first time he saw him, but he loved him when he died. (If one is looking for a martyr—which is to say, witness—in it all, to die at the hands of one you love, for a cause in which you believe strongly enough to let the beloved kill you, is coming mighty close.) If he had loved only those blacks with whom he lived and ate and worshiped, it might have been different. Then one might set up conditions and issue ultimatums in order to get mileage out of his death, in order to have his death "mean something." But since he loved his murderer, his death is its own meaning. And what that means is that his murderer is forgiven. If Jonathan forgives him, as he did when he came to love him, then it is not for me to cry for his blood. Any act on my part which is even akin to "avenging" his death is sacrilege. Vengeance negates martyrdom. It never confirms it. The sacramental act was Jonathan's, not mine.

When he loved his killer he set him free, for that is what love is. We might at least have learned that much from 2,000 years of punishing Jews for killing Christ.

But apart from that, for the Christian to invoke the law of the State in this case is as absurd as it would have been for the early Christians to have gone to court following the death of Polycarp in 155, or for the Gospel Missionary Union to have lobbyed for a war with Ecuador when Nathaniel Saint was killed at the hands of a savage Jinaro Indian mob in 1958. Clearly, Jonathan was as much a missionary as Nathaniel. And any time a Christian is set apart and sent forth to proclaim the bold and offensive *Word*, death is apt to be the outcome. While no one can find it within himself to rejoice in this death, we at least must know that what happened was the worst that they could do, that all Satan can produce is death, and that that enemy has been conquered by *The Word*. If Jonathan's murderer had understood this, he would have seen his act as one of folly. But knowing well the law, it made a lot of sense.

Of course, in all our demands for more law, we are insistent that what we are working for is a society in which this will not happen again. But even that is troublesome. We feel comfortable enough working and marching for a society in which a man can vote, go to school, ride a bus, buy a house, get a job or burn his draft card. But somehow we are not quite so comfortable working toward *a State* that will defend God against those who stone his prophets.

Perhaps to be stoned is the only witness we have left.

And might the truth of the matter be that we don't quite—not yet quite after all this time and all our learning and theologizing and all our protestation of faith—trust the central theme of the Gospel, the triumph of grace over law?

The notion that a man can go to a store where a group of unarmed human beings are assembled, fire a shotgun blast at one of them, tearing his lungs and heart and bowels from his body, turn on another and send lead pellets ripping through his flesh and bones, and that God will set him free is almost more than we can stand. But unless that is precisely the case, then there is no Gospel, there is no Good News. Unless that is the truth we are back under law, and Christ's death and resurrection are of no account.

When a man kills, he commits a crime against the state. The state, for reasons of its own, may choose not to punish him for that crime against itself.

When a man kills, he commits a crime against God. The strange, the near maddening thing about this case is that both these offended parties have rendered the same verdict—not for the same reasons, not in the same way, but the verdict is the same—acquittal.

The Christian response here is not to damn "acquittal by law," but to proclaim, in Markus Barth's phrase, "acquittal by *resurrection*." The one frees him to go and kill again. The other liberates him for obedience to Christ. Acquittal by law was the act of Caesar. Render unto him what is his. The State, by its very nature and definition, does whatever it wills to do—Hitler proved that much. Acquittal by resurrection was the act of God. And he has entrusted the Christian with that message.

A crime was also committed against Jonathan. And Jonathan rendered a similar verdict—acquittal—when he loved him.

But that murderer also committed an offense against us, against those of us churchmen who set Jonathan apart and sent him forth. Thus far we have come out worst of all.

Perhaps it is because we are afraid of the racists of this world. Perhaps it is because they rebuffed us in the Delta and elsewhere. But worse than either of these, it may be that we just plain do not love them.

The blood that is on our hands is more than that of Daniels and Reeb, Schwerner and Lee, Cheney and Goodman, Evers, Jackson, and King. The blood that is on our hands is the immortal souls of all racists who committed crimes against their brothers, and did so in the name of Jesus Christ.

That makes them blasphemers. If we, the righteous ones, the children of light, can offer them only law for their deliverance, we are approaching the point of joining them in that offense.

If he persists in his blasphemy, and we in ours, we may yet be integrated with him—but integrated in hell. What then have we *overcome?*

A few years ago a civil rights leader said to a group of whites, "If I come into a restaurant and sit down near you, I don't care if you vomit in your plate. Just don't keep me from sitting there." This is understandable. This may even be what simple justice is about, and let us not minimize its importance. But it falls far short of the reconciliation effected by a crucified God.

That *Event,* that *Word,* assures his right to the table because it abolished such worldly categories as race. And it stops the vomiting in the plate. That is what reconciliation is about. That is what God has done. Immanuel.

III
Deceptive Words

Thus says the Lord of hosts, the God of Israel, Amend your ways and your doings, and I will let you dwell in this place. Do not trust in these deceptive words: "This is the temple of the Lord, the temple of the Lord, the temple of the Lord." ... Behold, you trust in deceptive words to no avail. Will you steal, murder, commit adultery, swear falsely, burn incense to Baal, and go after other gods that you have not known, and then come and stand before me in this house, which is called by my name, and say, "We are delivered!"—only to go on doing these abominations? Has this house, which is called by my name, become a den of robbers in your eyes? Behold, I myself have seen it, says the Lord.

(Jeremiah 7, 1-4. 8-10)

Jeremiah warned Israel (the People of God) about trusting in the "deceptive words" that a religious institution ought to be worshiped for the deliverance it promises in its own strength. Yet trust in just such deceptive words is exactly what is happening in and to churches today. We trust in the "deceptive words" that churches are the ground for their own existence, that the churches' first duty is to themselves, that church structures may become disorganized and irrelevant but never perverted, and that churches authenticate their own existence, justify their own activities and sanctify whatever may be the activities of their members. By churches we are talking not only about buildings and people coming together once or twice a week (except June-August) for sundry matters which may or may not include worship and thanksgiving. We mean also the institutionalized temples, those tentacles of boards and agencies and bureaus that have grown into ends in themselves, into gods to be served by parson and layman alike, and that, on occasion, demand human sacrifice from those who publicly express doubts of their divinity. We are, in other words, talking about what Jeremiah meant by the deception of "the temple"—institutions which equate their existence with the life of God, institutions which claim the authority to proclaim by their own authority and in their own strength, "We are delivered!"

What are the consequences of our trust in these "deceptive words"? Almost daily the office of the Committee of Southern Churchmen is called upon by preachers who are being pressured out of their ministry, preachers who feel they are no longer able to say, do, and be what seems to be expected of them by those who bear a large share of responsibility for financially and socially supporting their efforts to proclaim the Gospel. Beyond trying to get them a "job," one frankly does not know what to "do," and, still less, what to "say." But whatever needs to be said must be said about us all, for we have all trusted the deceptive words.

The haplessness of the churches in what the world refers to as "social issues" is the most evident expression of trust in the deceptive words—words which in fact and in deed contradict the Source of life in the Church. The failure of the churches on the "race" question springs from the same misplaced trust as the sin of the churches on matters of politics, war, poverty, hunger and misery, and is warp and woof of the idolatry of the churches' attempt to sanctify their agencies, buildings, and business enterprises. Our willingness to grant that in the body of Christ there is such a thing as "race" springs from the same misplaced trust as our unwillingness to equate God with all men in the sense of Immanuel, God-with-us; and these, in turn, are warp and woof of the human sacrifice we exact from our ministers, seminary and college teachers, laymen, and youth because they refuse to trust the "deceptive words: 'This is the temple of the Lord, the temple of the Lord, the temple of the Lord.'"

The victims of the churches' trust in deceptive words about "the Church and race" are more numerous, perhaps, than even the most cynical observer might suspect. Often such a victim simply "leaves the ministry" rather than subject friends and family to the agony of a public airing of what he knows in his heart will be their trial: the *"they* have *their* churches, we have *ours;* why should we 'go out after them' when they are perfectly content with *their* own churches and the way they do things in them; after all, a church is for worship, not for socializing and politicking."

Deceptive words! And what does a man do with and say about the time and the talents he has invested in years—even decades—in the ministry when even the smallest of multitudes will hear him no longer? What shall he do with himself and with others when he has made his last "talk" to the liberal-minded group, and writes his last "article" on "the Church and race"? What does he do with and say about all this to his family, his friends, his God? Of course, there is the Poverty Program, and VISTA, and the Human Rights Commissions, and institutional and military chaplaincies, and the staff of the Justice Department, and insurance, possibly even a graduate degree and a teaching career somewhere in some discipline (except "religion," where there is scarcely a seller's market), or there are "education" courses at the state university, accreditation, and the public school system. What else can one say to them?

Equally if not more depressing—and undoubtedly more numerous—are the victims of those temple autocrats who trust in the "deceptive words" that Church agencies are self-justifying. Here, the "race" issue, or "Birchism," or even religious "orthodoxy" seldom if ever is at stake, for a self-justifying institution will not permit "either/or" issues to come to the surface. They are "dealt with in committee." Instead, the churches and their agencies authenticate themselves as a sort of special preserve of the good things and services and comforts and conveniences of *this* life that go to "them who are called" into the service of the Church, agency or bureau. More parsons than we dare think—young and otherwise—pack their grips and leave Church and ministry heartsick and physically nauseated at the sanctimonious, self-righteous, material aggrandizement by agency and individual that is part and parcel of the cult of trusting in the deceptive words that lead churches to live for themselves instead of their Lord. One hears of such incidents of aggrandizement and raw ambition and is reminded of those foes Paul faced in the congregation at Corinth, who insisted that the resurrection age was already at hand, thus liberating the true believer to all things material, sensual, and what have you. Or one sees a paraphrase of the attitude of a churchman of another era, "The Lord has given us the church offices; let us enjoy them!"

What does such a victim of the autocrats of deceptive words do and say about the time and talent invested in his years—even decades—in the ministry? What shall he *now* do with himself and with others—those who "quit," and who have made no "talks" about their experiences to the liberal-minded organizations, and written no "articles" for the prophetic journals? What shall he do with and say about all this to his family, his friends, his God, this victim who could no longer turn his head away from crass and overt perversions of the mission of the Church?

And what does the layman do who listens in vain for a Word other than what he hears on TV and reads in the newspaper? What does a youth do who sees not the pragmatism and wholesomeness but the chicanery and duplicity of the secular city celebrated in microcosm in the household which offers itself as the body of that man whose "purpose in dying for all was that men, while still in life, should cease to live for themselves, and should live for him who for their sake died and was raised to life"? And, most important of all, what do those do who "labor and are heavy laden," the ones who are promised "rest"? In God's name, what do we all do when the prophet's warning that we trust in deceptive words "to no avail" is sealed in the blood and resurrection of Christ?

Paul's answer appears simplistic, naive and unrealistic,

but here it is: "It is not ourselves that we proclaim; we proclaim Christ Jesus as Lord, and ourselves as your servants, for Jesus' sake. For the same God who said, 'Out of darkness let light shine,' has caused his light to shine within us, to give the light of revelation—the revelation of the glory of God in the face of Jesus Christ" (2 Cor. 4, 5-6). The deceptive word we proclaim is ourselves; we live for ourselves, we trust in ourselves. But all this is to "no avail" if Jeremiah and Paul are true in their witness to the Word that defines "deceptive words"; the "light" that "we proclaim" is not there and does not shine because of our achievements and our trust in ourselves, but because God "has caused his light to shine within us."

Patently, the Church is an institution whose structures, groupings, interests and values can (and should) be studied by those skilled in and enthusiastic about such analyses. Paul says as much: "We are no better than pots of earthenware to contain this treasure." Hence, the Church has no immunity from all the temptations which beset the finite and the sinful, and it is occasionally pleasant and reassuring to have the experts document this for us in their own idiom. But the point is that when we of the Church deny or overlook the earthenware quality of the Church, when we confuse or even equate pots of earthenware with the treasure the pots have been commissioned to carry—*not possess, only carry!*—we trust in deceptive words, and to no avail! We proclaim ourselves, not Christ Jesus as Lord, but to no avail! We live for ourselves and our temples of deceptive words and not for the poor, the prisoner, the blind, the frightened, the desperate, the racist, the autocrat, the harlot, the haughty, the prideful—those, in a word, to whom Christ came and for whom he died and raised to life. Patently again, whatever institutional reordering may be demanded because we trusted in deceptive words will not spring from sociological analyses and projections, but from a renewal, a repentance, a "rightwising" that takes place within the fellowship of those individuals who proclaim "Christ Jesus as

Lord, and ourselves as your servants, for Jesus' sake." Nowhere in the New Testament is there a guarantee that the churches may not on occasion have to abandon, or even reject, the institutional temples which become the focus of the temptation to trust in deceptive words, and thereby deny Christ Jesus as Lord. Jesus' own cleansing of the temple was not done once and for all time. And just this specifically is Paul's proclamation about the task and mission of the Church and the source of the renewal of that task and mission—namely that not we, but God, renews: "We are not better than pots of earthenware to contain this treasure, and this proves that such transcendent power does not come from us, but is God's alone" (2 Cor. 4, 7).

Something is going on in our midst, but we cannot yet discern too clearly the significance or the direction. The temples that trust in deceptive words are being cleansed, but now, as then, by Christ Jesus. We may be entering (or more accurately, returning to) an era in which salaried workers will decrease, and perhaps perform purely technical functions, in which certain bureaucracies and organizations of the churches will become increasingly integrated into the welfare activities of society, and in which new congregations will arise which will not judge who they are by "worldly standards" or the size of their membership, or even pay much attention to where and when they gather to worship and praise God, provided that they do so scripturally, in word *and deed,* and therefore during all the other hours and days and weeks when they are in the field.

What if the offices and bureaus and agencies and services —the structures and institutions—of the body of Christ became by God's grace the "pots of earthenware" containing this "treasure" of witness of Christ Jesus as Lord? What if the "treasure" became the center of our trust and proclamation to such an extent that successful temples were measured by how effectively they went out of business to make way for new structures and institutions? What if it is even true that where only two or three are gathered together in a ghetto hovel, or a plush basement, or a suburban living room, or a 'cropper's shack, or a hillbilly's hillside, or a tenement, or a brush arbor, or a dormitory—but gathered together, nevertheless, in his name—he is in the midst of them?

Why not? "We are no better than pots of earthenware to contain this treasure, *and this proves that such transcendent power does not come from us, but is God's alone.*"

IV
Footwashing or the New Hermeneutic?

What will the racial situation be in the churches of the South when the Yankees have all gone home? They said they came because we had done so little. We may question the conjunction, but not the assertion on either side of it. They *did* come. And we *had* done so little.

How short a time ago it was that they came! We had heard the talk of the long, hot summer. Then they came. Several of them we killed. Then the rest went away. At least most of them went away, though none to our knowledge went away because we killed several of them. Most stayed longer because of that.

How short a time ago it was that the Ivy League doctors —mostly the teaching, preaching doctors, but a few of the doctoring doctors—were here. There were the calls to take them bail or to visit them. Was it Birmingham, Montgomery, Albany, or Jackson? Was it Freedom Ride, Voter Registration, or Sit-in? Anyway, they were here and we were glad, and now they are gone. Sometimes one hears that they are a part of the Clergy Concerned with the War in Vietnam—a worthy cause, God knows, but how fickle they are, our Yankee brothers.

They came to be our conscience because we let expectant citizens be shot down in the streets and little girls be slaughtered at their prayers. But conscience is not a thing of the moment. It is a thing of generations. It could not be remade in one summer or two.

There was the Mississippi Project, the F.D.P. and COFO, baptized in Oxford, Ohio, and confirmed somewhere between there and Neshoba County where three at once were buried in the red clay of a government dam.

Surely such an offspring would last for a long time. But it didn't. It is true that a law was passed, and then another; and now a third is proposed after Wallace showed us once more what we should have known all along about the South, and while senators tell us what we should have known about the North —"Any further legislation is clearly unconstitutional on its face." (Southern rednecks are one thing. Northern rentals are another.)

Meanwhile there were more than twenty race-related murders in the South in a one-year period following the Civil Rights Act of 1964, making that the bloodiest since the Movement began.

And yet they have all gone away. At least almost all of them. And surely their dream is gone—the dream that the Mississippi Project, the F.D.P. and COFO would arouse that latent goodness supposed to be in all men, Southern and Federal, and that we would rise up to stay the evil passion of racism. That dream is gone. From that we have awakened. The dream of a degree of justice remains, and thank God. That is an important dream. But the dream of reconciliation based on the coming of the Yankees is gone. If one does not believe it, then let him go to a tavern in Tennessee and hear the manager say, following the visit of a thirsty black man, "Yes, we have to serve them, but we break every glass they drink out of. There is no law against that." That may be justice, but it is not reconciliation. Or let him go into a truck stop with a black friend and watch the waitress stroll casually to the juke box. Hear her dime produce the words, sung to well-composed and equally well-played music;

> Move them niggers north.
> Move them niggers north.
> If they don't like our Southern ways,
> Move them niggers north.

There is no law against playing the juke box. Not yet. To say nothing about the dangers of having one.

Where is the reconciliation? In fact, where is the justice? Is there really any justice in a hamburger? Or does the juke box negate even the hamburger, for who could hold it down? Anyway, most of them are gone. SNCC—though not really North—remains, but since they recently declared their intention of becoming all black, their dream of "beloved community" becomes a spasm—at least for white churchly folk. And the Delta Ministry remains in name, but days after their Poor People's Conference sought to take over the Greenville Air Base, a faction of that Conference sought to take over the leased property of the Delta Ministry *at gunpoint!* Folks don't like such ingrates as that, especially if the enthusiasm and financial support from back home are on the wane. The Freedmen's Bureau, one of the more promising programs to come South following the Civil War, folded after six years. It did so because the lack of financial support discouraged its advocates to the point of giving up. A very similar thing is happening now, and we may anticipate an early departure of those whom some saw as hostile invaders and others regarded as our last hope. Who then will remain?

We will. We who were born here, who partly created and partly fell heir to what we have come to call "the race problem." Black and white, Christian, Jew, and pagan, we remain. And we will remain. If anyone does.

And what hope is there among *us?* There are indigenous black groups and interracial organizations to which we can still look for help. Help, but not Messiah. Even the all-black policy of many may be at once judgment and long-range hope. Those individuals now involved, however, may see the promised land of true reconciliation (which they verbally reject but still yearn to see) only from an isolated mountain, standing there alone, with neither leader nor follower. Though wrought with so many internal problems that the sophisticated white liberal sees little hope, they may yet be the tailor for the sackcloth and ashes which we continue to shun, but which remains the only acceptable garment for an audience with the Almighty.

But what hope is there among us, within us, the Church? If by that one means the institution, after forty years within it we sadly conclude—*none!* For there is little to indicate that we are any different today from what we were in 1954, in 1964, and in 1969. If we see the all-black policy of SNCC as the hardened heart which God uses as his judgment upon a segment, then we, the churches, may be the hardened heart which he uses as judgment upon us all.

If we are to be honest, we must admit that at the congregational level the white church in the South has not yet had the slightest involvement in the racial crisis. A few pastors have joined an occasional march. A few more have signed statements. But the fact is that most of these do not march or sign statements or serve as pastors any longer; their flocks not only did not follow them to street and parchment, but they did not tolerate the controversy resulting from their shepherds' strange behavior. If the drought of direct action has been acute during the past few years, the drought of preaching is chronic. Embarrassed with the "Bible Belt" label that the Fundamentalists have caused us to bear, most of us theological sophisticates have shied away from a doctrine of man rooted deeply in Scripture, the doctrine which rejects race as a category. Instead, we have turned to the more scientific and neutral documentation for such preaching as we have done on the subject. Our flocks have rejected social analysis and political meddling as none of the preachers' business—as they should have done (though their reasons were wrong)—so that our congregations have been left to flounder in the mire of religion—the curse of man which Christ sought to dispel, but which continues to dominate us in such proportion as to approach anti-Christ.

But let us not speak now of the churches. Let us speak now of churchmen. Let us confess that we failed to admit the frailty of institutions from the beginning. Had we done so,

Footwashing or the New Hermeneutic? 43

we would not now sink into despair about the inadequacies of the institutional Church. And it is no good to talk now of "para-Church." Whatever ways for witness we may find as Christians will be the witness of *Church*, or it will not be witness at all.

And there are at least two embarrassments which we must overcome. The first is the embarrassment of biblicism. The second is the embarrassment of the sects. They may well be treated together.

Partly because we rejected Fundamentalism as adolescents (and the seminaries gave us a sounder basis of criticism to sustain the rejection), and partly because we saw the evils of institutionalized biblical literalism, we turned away from seeking answers in the Scriptures. While the religious racists have indoctrinated the South with biblical distortions, we theologically-trained sophisticates retreated into . . . the New Hermeneutic! No one will deny that a hook and ladder is better equipment for fighting a fire than a garden hose. But the house is on fire. There is no time to send to Detroit for hooks and ladders. There is no time to await scholarly research—unless, of course, we will enjoy the Stoic satisfaction of consoling ourselves, as observers, that the fire might have been put out long after the embers are dead.

The point is a simple one. Everything else has failed. There has been no reconciliation. There has been precious little social change. Remember how we used to scoff at the "moderates" when they said, "What they are doing will set race relations back fifty years!" We should still be dubious of this and all other clichés. But it is more and more obvious that the social changes have not seen a corresponding change in the basic human relationships of one man to another—black to white and white to black. Such interpersonal relationships are not considered important by those who see the change of the structures as our greatest hope. But structures are persons, groups of persons, who lean in the same direction at a given point in history, just as presidents, senators, and Supreme Court justices read the morning paper to learn the direction in which their followers are leaning.

And although it is denied by both groups, white liberals are cooling off at a rapid pace, and a considerable element of the civil rights movement is moving pell-mell into the yawning lap of Black Nationalism. Thousands who referred to the justice, rightness, and necessity of the Selma March of 1965 are now referring to the "Sweet Willie Wine" 1969 Memphis to Little Rock March as a civil rights williwaw without meaning or purpose. Yet, we fail to see the difference if either had to do with injustice, for there was as much injustice on the road from Memphis to Little Rock in 1969 as there was from Selma to Montgomery in 1965.

And the denominational commissions on race are roughly back where they were four years ago—passing resolutions deploring this or that, and urging individual church members to wire the President.

Great God Almighty!

What does, what could, what will, the President of the United States ever have to do with the witness of the Church? And when will we quit seeing him as our spiritual head?

Why are we back where we were after those exciting years of more or less active participation in the Movement? The answer again is simple. More and more white folks are seeing that the Movement is not about coffee and hamburgers, or black and white together, but rather is about a more equitable distribution of the goods and opportunities that whites have simply because they are white. And more and more Movement leaders don't want whites involved because they don't, they can't, trust them. In 1965 all the Established Church groups were issuing nationwide appeals for marchers to go to Selma. There were no such appeals in 1966 for participation in the Mississippi marches. There were some tactical reasons offered, but the real, the big reason was that those appeals in 1965 resulted in too many white folks who marched and dominated the march. If there is one prophetic role the National Councils' commissions and departments of Christian social relations can play now, it is to tell white Christians the truth, however painful and unpopular it might be: Stay home! Anyone who was surprised with the Black Power development must never have read the Bible or history, for the development began when the first slave ship departed the shores of Africa.

But enough of saying things are worse. Actually things are not worse for everyone. We are not saying that. Things are better for a fairly large number of blacks. Things are also better for a fairly large number of whites, for *they* are better off, economically. The recent civil rights legislation and the Office of Economic Opportunity programs have had some effect within the culture. Not much, but some.

When we speak of things being worse, we are talking of institutionalized Christianity being worse. It is worse simply because it is not better. It is not better because it remained where it was twenty, ten, two years ago, protective of its own, self-loving and largely self-worshiping, while the world whirled by.

So where do we turn? One thing that all other institutions have learned from the civil rights movement is that the very structures which they assumed to be sacred were not sacred after all. Restaurant owners learned that there was nothing as sacred about property rights as they had thought. School boards are learning that there is nothing as sacred about, neighborhood schools as they had thought. ("If you can go to the moon, you can bus our children across town.") Only the churches continue to insist that their structures are sacred. As long as they are sacred, they will be stagnant and sterile. A sacred tool is one not to be used but to be fondled and polished. Howard Moody says the Church is an instrument of God literally to be used up in his service, a service to those not even within it. There is little evidence at this point in God's economy of the Church going out of business through such usefulness.

But there has been a segment of the Church whose idols have been less secure than main-line, white Protestantism. These have been what we call the fringe churches, the sects. And what do they do that others don't? Well, they wash one another's feet, they shout, they sing jazzed-up songs to guitar music, they handle snakes. They do all sorts of things. But *what* they do is not so important for our concern as the zeal with which they do it. They do it with zeal because they really believe it. And since they really believe in what they do, the tools they employ are not so important for them. A silver basin is fine for washing feet, but a galvanized foot tub is just as good. A brick, air-conditioned building is all right for handling snakes, but a brush arbor is just as good. Acoustical tile would be dandy for shouting, but an unpainted frame ceiling is just as good.

But aside from those things they do, a case can be made that they were more faithful in the racial crisis all along than the established Church.

Consider Horace Germany. Horace, a white man, had lived all his life in rural Neshoba County, Mississippi. He made his living by farming. He was also a Church of God preacher. Ten years ago we saw him for the first time. He was lying on his side, his back purple and sore from a beating he had just received from his neighbors. He told this story only after a letter of introduction was shown to him, written by a Church of God preacher in another state.

He had wanted to build a school for Church of God young people who had been called to preach. He would teach them tentmaking, of whatever variety they chose. They would study the Bible, and they would do it without regard to race, for he said he believed that the Gospel was a "universal Gospel to all men, as given by Christ in the Great Commission. All men are made one in Jesus Christ."

To reach his school, it was necessary to drive down a country dirt road which came very near the scene where some years later three civil rights workers were to be murdered and buried.

Footwashing or the New Hermeneutic? 47

About three miles down that recently graded, winding and sloping dirt road, hardly wide enough for two cars to pass, there was an open gate at the top of the slope. Through the wooded area there was a clearing and a large pond, the kind the U.S. Department of Agriculture builds for farmers to water cattle. Beside the pond was a long shed with lumber stacked almost to the tin roof. Outside the shed were more lumber and concrete blocks, some with black mildew and spider webs, indicating that this building material had been accumulated over an extended period of time. In the center of the clearing there was the foundation and part of the first story of a large building. This was the beginning of the school.

And it was the beginning of Horace Germany's troubles. A week earlier a large crowd—including, no doubt, some blood cousins as well as Christian brothers of ours—had gathered at one of the main-line churches in the area. Some two hundred could be accommodated inside, and another estimated five hundred formed a sea of solemn faces on the dry, dusty lawn and pressed as closely as possible to open doors and windows in order not to miss the important proceedings inside.

There were the customary prayers which must precede any event in church, but a minimum of preliminaries. They were there to discuss the school construction down the road. A resolution was presented, discussed, and then adopted with a voice vote consisting of shouts—shouts not generally heard in the services of that denomination. The resolution asserted that the school was seeking to destroy harmony between the white and colored races of the area. "The college is purportedly a Christian educational institution," the resolution stated, but, "we are convinced that the purpose of this college is to promote, foster, and encourage violence and to disrupt the good will between the races."

Following the meeting at the church a committee of two hundred waited upon Brother Germany and delivered this message: "Preacher, this is it! We mean, this is it! You get your family and them imported niggers (he already had several students) away from here within forty-eight hours, or we will not be responsible for what happens." Horace reported wryly that "liquor and tobacco smelled strongly, and some of them talked rough."

The newsletter which they mailed regularly to friends and supporters reported the events that followed:

> On Friday, August 26, Pres. Germany, Vice Pres. Burns, and three of our brethren drove into Union where we had bought part of a school building. They were loading material onto the truck when a mob of five or six carloads came, drove the Colored brethren away at the threat of their lives, and set into beating Bro. Germany in a most unmerciful manner with blackjacks, fists, clubs, and while he was on the ground they would kick him. It was one of the most outrageous things that has happened since the establishment of any form of law and order in the United States, especially in connection with the activity of the Church. At this writing Bro. Germany is still in the hospital.

He talked sadly of his shattered dream. We asked him what he planned to do. He said that he wasn't afraid. "Jesus died for me, and I will die for him. I could finish the school all right. People from all over the country have said they would bring their trailers and tents and stand guard until the school is finished. But all I would prove is that I am not afraid. I could build the buildings, but it wouldn't be a school. There would be no students. A school is not a school without students."

"And what will you do with what you have built?"

He turned slowly away and gazed steadily at the wall. A plaster of paris plaque, looking at once like those won at county fair carnivals and the kind made by children at vacation Bible schools, hung on the wall with the inscription: "In all thy ways acknowledge him, and he will direct thy path."

"Yesterday morning one of the biggest bootleggers in the county sent word that he wanted to buy the property. I know

Footwashing or the New Hermeneutic? 49

what he wants with it. He wants to make a dance hall out of my school and sell whiskey."

"And will you sell it to him?"

"Yes," he said. "Yes, I'm going to sell it to him. I told these people that if they won't let God do his work in this county, the Devil will sure move in and do his. There's a lot more to this race problem than just segregation."

And how right he was. Maybe those who killed Mickey and James and Andy in Neshoba County that night got the courage to do it in a bottle from what began as the Bay Ridge Christian College.

There were numerous others from the sects who have been both prophetic and courageous in the racial crisis. There was James Willis Vaughn, a tall, raw-boned preacher from one of the most rigidly Fundamentalistic sects, who preached a revival at Bethlehem Temple in Jackson, and because the host under whose roof he slept was black, he was fined five hundred dollars, and he and his wife spent sixty days in jail.

But the point for us is not who they were and what they did, but what *we* can learn from *them*.

We are not suggesting that we turn seminaries into training centers for learning to handle copperheads and wash one another's feet—though if Aubrey Norvel would wash James Meredith's feet, and Meredith would let him do it, we would be for setting Norvel free.

The real point is that the idols of the sects are not as secure as those of the established Church. When the Yankees have all gone home, this may be the hope for renewal if we in the Establishment can learn to . . . Think Sect!

And what does "Think Sect" mean? It means brush arbors and communion on a kitchen table. It means preaching on street corners and baptizing in a mill pond or out of a coffee cup. It means Clarence Jordan buried in a pine box in south Georgia. It means Tom Merton's Masses at the hermitage in Nelson County, Kentucky, and the Berrigans' Masses and baptisms in living rooms and in the corners of Protestant chapels and in the streets.

It means poverty. The institutional Church stands today exactly where the rich young ruler stood in Matthew 19 (and it stands before the same Lord). He was rich, he was powerful, he was good. The Church is rich. It is powerful. And it is good. No one ever calls it bad. It is high on the list of agencies to do good in the community when the need arises. The United Givers Fund, the Boy Scouts, the Lions International, the Red Cross, the Church—each will accept its quota of responsibility. Yet the reply of our Lord was to get rid of all that and then come and be a disciple.

Think Sect means carrying a cyanide capsule in your navel against the day the enemy is so strong against you that the only way you can preserve that with which you have been entrusted is to kill yourself. The enemy is now that strong against us. The enemy has made us rich, powerful and good, knowing that when there was a racial crisis or a Vietnam war, the best we would risk would be debates and resolutions and petitions. The cyanide capsule tucked in our navel is Matthew 19. Let us now swallow it with a joyful gulp. Sell the steeples, the organs, the gold cups, the silver hats, the mahogany pews and the valuable downtown property and give the money away. Give it to BEDC, to the Fentress Low Income People (FLIP), to the poor in the Ku Klux Klan, or simply to those of the poor who happen to be nigh. Don't ask if they are from the deserving or the undeserving poor. Just give it away.

And Think Sect. Then shout Hallelujah! Then sing the psalms. Then *follow!* But above all, remember that with that one act, Jesus did not offer to the rich young ruler the end of discipleship. That act only qualified him to approach the starting line of discipleship.

Think Sect.

V
Milestones into Millstones

Many milestones in the racial crisis have occurred during the past decade, and we who consider ourselves the children of light have rejoiced in them. We have seen movements, political activity, legislation, court decisions, historic gatherings that symbolized longed for and anticipated hope, and we were encouraged. The milestones gave us renewed courage, and from time to time we would gather to rededicate our talents, renew our strength and pledge the continuation of our efforts.

Today, as we consider the milestones in the context of recent happenings, we are confused and alarmed.

"What do 'they' want now?" is the question of the day. "They" wanted to ride in the front of the bus and we gave them another series of decisions. "They" wanted to eat in the restaurant of their choice and we gave them a Civil Rights Act. So now what is the trouble?

"The trouble, dear Cassius, is not in our stars but in ourselves that we are underlings." The trouble is that we keep asking the question: "What can *we* do now to make *you* happy, to keep *you* off the streets and off *our* backs?"

It is a question honestly asked. The only problem is that there is no answer to it. Or, if there is an answer, it is likely to be one word: *Nothing*.

Of all people Americans seem to be the hardest pressed to admit that there is a problem we cannot solve, that we have created something which we cannot now control, or destroy.

And of all people we seem to be the hardest pressed to acknowledge that in reality it is God's judgment we are facing, that it is apocalypse we are witnessing.

We do not claim the gift of prophecy. One leading American anthropologist has already suggested that even prophecy can be automated. "Each great university," she said, "should have a Chair of the Future." And already church folk and church magazines regularly hold conferences and distribute special issues to try to align us with the future—apparently unaware that Garner Ted Armstrong *et pere* ("The World Tomorrow!") have been on the radio for over thirty years. "The professor," our anthropologist explains, "would simply feed the computer provided by the university, and divulge its readings at regular intervals to the students."

At first glance this seems to relieve the People of God of the only responsibility they have not openly abdicated. Poverty, race, human relations, family affairs, sickness, morality of various sorts, education and many other things were once the business of the Church. Few see them as such any longer. And now apocalyptic interpretation is going to be handled by a machine. But the computer is not as threatening to us as it might seem. For the data fed into it can only be historical, based on precedents.

Thus we envision the Academic Man from U.N.C.L.E. facing his Ivy League class of tomorrow's magnates with the results of two semesters' feedings in his hand.

"And now, young people, the computer says that within three years after your graduation the world will cease to exist in anything but the most insignificant plant life."

This hardly creates a ripple, for the migration has already begun to the Housatonic River for the annual Derby Day. And they have heard this same message before, from the peace marchers.

But the professor is a thorough man. "Now you must understand, young people, that this includes General Motors, IBM, General Dynamics, Boeing Aircraft, Westchester County, and all of Boston. And you must understand that these are not the words of the preachers and pacifists but of the computer."

This does create a ripple. In fact there is bedlam that carries right through the bell to signal the end of the class. "All right, Mr. Prof. Now you just ask the damn thing what we must do. Ask it! Ask it! Ask it!"

"But," says the professor, "that will take another semester."

Well, some of them were meant to graduate, but the machine had said that the end included General Motors, IBM, General Dynamics, Boeing Aircraft, Westchester County, and all of Boston. So they were all back next semester.

Miltowns, amphetamines, LSD for the more nervous, kept them going while the appropriate data were fed into the machine. The Chair of the Future had become the only course attended. The chancellor of the university had been relegated to minding its auxiliary power station, the president emptied his urine bag, but the deans and department chairmen remained at work on the self-study project and revising curricula.

Then the day came and they were all there. The lights whirled in rhythmic patterns. The little bells clamored and chimed all at once, like every radio station in the nation introducing: "News! While it happens, every hour on the hour." The tape was finally deposited into the hands of the only calm man in the room—the professor.

As if he already knew the answer he turned and faced them.

"It says, 'REPENT!'"

If what we are facing is apocalyptic, what are the data? First of all we know that nothing has changed. We have the milestones—the 1954 Court decision and the '55, '56, '57, '58 and '59 supporting decisions outlawing one racist gimmick after another. We have Mrs. Rosa Parks who, because her feet hurt, would not move to the back of the bus, and we have the Montgomery Improvement Association which that act set off. We have the milestone of 1960—the Sit-in Movement and the organization of SNCC. We have the Washington

March, the Civil Rights Act of 1964 and the Civil Rights Act of 1965, etc.

But despite the milestones, nothing has changed in the relationship between black people and white people.

Or perhaps it is *because* of the milestones that nothing has changed, for milestones have a strange way of becoming millstones. Have the milestones become millstones around the neck of American society, pulling it deeper and deeper into the sea which its past sins have created? White America keeps pointing to the milestones: "But look at what we have done." And black America keeps pointing to them as millstones and saying, "Yes, look. Look at what you have done."

Milestones become millstones in apocalyptic terms when they become a source of pride instead of a source of penitence, when the uniform announcing them is red, white and blue alpaca and not coarse sackcloth.

Milestones become millstones in apocalyptic terms when they are celebrated more by the donor than by the recipient. And it is white people who tell the world of our gains, not black people.

What can we say when black and white glare at each other and threaten and attack each other across the chasm not bridged but widened by politics and law? We can begin by looking at some of the political and legal milestones.

Begin with the 1954 Court decision outlawing segregation in the public schools. Each year we see the statistics, well documented and researched, from the Southern Education Reporting Service, or second-hand from the U.S. Office of Education. They tell of how many new black children have shown up in previously all-white schools. They do not tell what happens to them when they arrive. And we do not have to go to Grenada, Mississippi, and see the little children stalked and beaten with chains intended to harness mules to turning plows, nor to Plaquemine Parish, Louisiana, and hear the chant of "nigger, nigger, nigger" by the white majority or even, in some cases, minority. Perhaps, in a way, there is something redemptive to the victims of such blatant outrage as being beaten by trace chains. There is a sense in which they *can* love the perpetrators of such obvious wrong—it is easier to smile when a driver comes all the way over into your lane of traffic and smashes your car than it is when it is not quite clear just what happened. (Then everybody gets mad.)

The alleged newsworthiness of the child beatings has been sufficiently exaggerated as to blind us to the greater dangers of the subtleties which daily remind black children of their condition. It is news when he makes good grades, and it is true that most of the time he doesn't. The first high school in one state to desegregate still doesn't let black students play in the band. A junior high class is told never to elect a team of cheerleaders composed of a white girl and a black lad. (The teacher would be highly offended to be told she is a racist. Everything had "gone so well" at her school, she just didn't want to spoil the record.) Proms are discontinued because there might be trouble. And there are a hundred and one other little indignities that go to make up the seething cauldron of infection lying directly beneath the scar of racial desegregation.

It is little wonder that more and more black parents are saying, "We don't want desegregated schools. We want good schools." It is little wonder that the separatist position gets a greater hearing and following among black young people who have been exposed to desegregation than among their elders who never were.

This is not to argue against desegregation in schools. It is forward, not backward, that we must move. But we must be aware that the desegregated schools of the South today are roughly where the Michigan desegregated schools of Malcolm X's high school days were. His history teacher disposed of Negro history in one laughing, snickering, contemptuous sentence. It was not a rigid pattern of segregation that produced Malcolm X. It was a desegregated system in which he was thoroughly exposed to white sins. And it is probably no accident that practically all of the leading civil rights militants of our day have come out of such desegregated patterns— Malcolm X, Stokely Carmichael, Dick Gregory, Floyd McKissick and others.

Exposure can mean inoculation. Or it can mean catching

the disease. Those of us who have argued and worked for desegregation must have assumed that the injection of a few well-chosen and well-qualified blacks into the living organism called white society would stimulate the production of sufficient antibodies to deliver us from the deserved wrath of God and wrath of blacks. What would happen to the unchosen and unqualified did not seem to be a factor, the assumption being that *black* is the antigen and *white* is the living organism. The injection, however, did not immunize the alleged living organism against riots, poverty and racism. The well-dressed black man at the front desk of the savings-and-loan association and the well-mannered black athlete cured and prevented nothing.

And what if the final winners are the unchosen and the unqualified? And what will happen if they, like most victors of history, come to accept the gods of the vanquished—our gods? What if the unchosen and unqualified, now leaderless, find leaders from the ranks of those we are currently letting through the sieve, in the manner that leadership came to the African colonies from those the British educated?

These are two possibilities, depending on whether exposure to white produces immunity or disease. If immunity, the result could be the kind of health William Faulkner projected through Dilsey, the black cook, to a decaying and dying aristocratic family. If, instead, the white disease is caught, there is nothing to predict but an attempt at insurrection— an insurrection which will fail but perhaps only so long as it is national and not worldwide.

We have tried for several years now to avoid either possibility by widening the mesh in the strainer.

We will doubtless attempt to stay the attempt at insurrection in one of three ways.

1. Abolishing the sieve (and such concepts as "qualified") and determining that no one shall be naked, hungry or neglected.

2. Continuing to widen the sieve enough, at regular intervals, to keep the pressure beneath the blowup point.

3. Electing an apartheid President and Congress, slaughter-

ing or incarcerating those who oppose it, and thereby sealing our own doom in one final act of defiance and unfaith to the ruler of the universe. If this last alternative sounds absurd, we should remember that Hitler sounded equally absurd six months before he happened.

One can examine the milestones one by one and conclude that they are made of white clay, not black stone. The Civil Rights Act left the ghettos intact and the white suburbs safe. The Voting Rights Bill did encourage considerable numbers of black voters, but it also helped to ensure the election of several racist governors. The War on Poverty employed a small number of middle-class blacks and a much smaller number of poor blacks, but now it is on the verge of being phased out so that more black people can be killed in foreign (white) adventures.

Where are the millstones dragging us?

And if it is all apocalyptic, where does that leave the Church? What is God telling us in it all? Where and what is the sign? Where are God's people to stand?

Perhaps alongside the professor and his computer.

Because...

An evil and adulterous generation seeks for a sign, but no sign shall be given to it except the sign of Jonah.

VI
Politics as Baal

To suggest that "Repent!" is what the Church must "do" today—even in the company of the Ivy League professor from U.N.C.L.E.—immediately evokes all the specters of Billy Sunday, Billy Graham, Gypsy Smith, and Elmer Gantry. One is reminded of the very intense, very involved and very serious young church bureaucrat at a large ecumenical conference—concerned, as they say, with a pressing social problem—telling all who would listen, "If anyone says 'Repent!' at this meeting again, I'm going to vomit." The irony is that if someone had really laid out what the Bible meant by "Repent!" vomiting would have begun rather than finished his reaction—as well as the reaction of those who can always be counted on to attend churchly gatherings on pressing social issues.

For two decades now, we have chatted merrily and sometimes seriously—but with little appreciable result—about Bonhoeffer's warning that "cheap grace is the deadly enemy of the Church." Now let us take a look at repentance, the human pole, so to speak, of grace. Let us take heed of "cheap repentance"—which is to say, repentance which is not repentance at all, just as "cheap" grace is not grace at all. Let us center our considerations around the words of John the Baptist, "Bear fruits that befit repentance," and let our primary sources be Amos, Hosea, Isaiah and Jeremiah, seeking out what they have to say about this one question of repentance. Let us further remind ourselves that repentance is often translated "turn" or "return," emphasizing the radical, either/or, 180-degree, right-about-face quality of the *act* of repentance, the total, complete, and permanent reversal, by God, of one's life and being as well as one's thoughts—one's deeds as well as one's words—*from* the self and its idols *to* the God of Abraham, Isaac, Jacob, to God the Messiah, to Immanuel, God-with-us, Jesus Christ. And let us learn straightaway that if we regard the act with biblical seriousness, we are in the realm of the eschatological, the apocalyptic —that is, the moment when God confronts man to make repentance possible. Otherwise, Jesus is not Savior, but generous fellow, Paul is wrong and "Cephas" right (Galatians 2), Augustine a heretic and Pelagius a Father of the Church, Luther a psychologist and Erasmus a theologian, the Good News of the New Testament scientific and relevant and Hegel and Marshall McLuhan *skandalon*.

For repentance has nothing to do with functional reorganization and analysis; it is not another gimmick to meet the requirements of the cults of pietism, revivalism and relevance. It says nothing to general religious commitments or great moral requirements. Repentance is not beanbag. It is not scientific, modern, or relevant to our age. Beanbag, scientific analysis and the concern for relevance to our age masquerade as repentance. But when this happens, it is *too late* for repentance—a judgment under which our church institutions now stand: that is, our congregational structures, bureaus, agencies, colleges and seminaries. Consider Hosea—the prophet of *hesed*, of God's steadfast love, who is bound thereby to indict Israel for swearing, lying, killing, stealing, committing adultery, and murder upon murder (5, 4):

Their deeds do not permit them
   to return to their God.
For the spirit of harlotry is within them,
   and they know not the Lord.

What deeds created a structure—a *Gestalt*—of sin that led Israel to the point of no return, when *nothing* that Israel did could break the prison of evil that overwhelmed it? Harlotry. Baalism. Idolatry. Religion. Worshiping God with their lips, and worshiping themselves, their lusts, their ambitions, their activities, with their lives. Staking their exis-

Politics as Baal

tence on the finite, the temporal, the religious; celebrating, glorifying the secular; rejoicing in their culture; practicing the Baalism which so conveniently posed as a legitimate need (the problem of nature's cycles and caprice) and even more conveniently rationalized an illegitimate need (sexual lust and perversion). Consider the indictment and the punishment depicted in Hosea 10, 1-2; 8, 7-8; 6, 5-6:

> Israel is a luxuriant vine
>   that yields its fruit.
> The more his fruit increased
>   the more altars he built;
> as his country improved
>   he improved his pillars.
> Their heart is false;
>   now they must bear their guilt.
> The Lord will break down their altars,
>   and destroy their pillars.
>
> For they sow the wind,
>   and they shall reap the whirlwind.
> The standing grain has no heads,
>   it shall yield no meal;
> if it were to yield,
>   aliens would devour it.
> Israel is swallowed up;
>   already they are among the nations
>   as a useless vessel.
>
> Therefore I have hewn them by the prophets,
>   I have slain them by the words of my mouth,
>   and my judgment goes forth as the light.
> For I desire steadfast love and not sacrifice,
>   the knowledge of God, rather than burnt offerings.

The fact is, our deeds *never* permit us to return to God, to repent; otherwise, we would be saved by works—in which case we must do more than demythologize the Bible to preserve the relevance of the Christian faith. If we are able to turn ourselves to God, if we are able to save ourselves in our own strength and cleverness, then Jesus was a model, not the Messiah, and repentance is nothing more than the occasion, at hymn-time, responsive reading or prayer-time (every head bowed, every eye closed), to say, "I'm sorry, God, truly sorry that I am like I am and do what I do. But consider how great thou art, consider how weak I am, and you will surely understand: there is my business, my wife and oldest son, my colleagues and neighbors, the mortgage, my nerves, the communist menace, and then there is this woman. . . ."

And the fact is, of course, that he does "understand." That is why repentance is as it is and not the great "I'm sorry" which we would like it to be. That is why repentance is God's initiative in turning us right-about-face so that the *Gestalt* of evil can be overcome. That is why repentance is not World Communion Sunday or Race Relations Sunday, or the call made some years ago by a television religious personality (*not* Dr. Graham) for "national repentance." This masquerades repentance as the great "I'm sorry" of the lips while one determinedly remains locked firmly in place and headed in the same old direction toward destruction. To repent is not to establish a Commission on Social and Cultural Relations (the ecumenical euphemism for doing-something-about-our-Negro-brother-and-the-race-problem), for that is to extend the *Gestalt* of irresponsibility which permits the professionals—the ones who make a living at it, the ministers, the teachers, the priests, the agency men, the social workers —to become involved and to say in our place at the mass meetings and marches, "I'm sorry *you're black,*" and to go on—every one of us—as before. That is a diversion if not an outright denial of the life of evangelism. To repent is not Emergency Committees on Vietnam (as urgent and as overdue as they are), for that would be for the Committees to say, "I'm sorry" to the millions of victims—to the little ones, the innocent, the poor, the babies—for our *de facto* sanctification of every war for more centuries than we dare count. That is a denial in practice of the resurrection of Christ.

How is it possible in this 20th century, after the life, execution and return to life of Jesus Christ, for us to participate in all seriousness in the repentance found in the shenanigans and subterfuge of Committees on Social Action, the six-point grading program, biennial revivals, fierce onslaughts against drinking and smoking and pot and LSD, study committees and pamphlets on The Church, Cybernation and the Age of Tomorrow, the miserable and mandatory and sometimes heretical religious emphasis on the racist Christian campus, and holy communion of coke-and-chips to the beat of the Monkees? The answer will not be found in another institutional self-analysis, another study of the habits of the minister and of theological education, another inquiry into the missionary structure of the congregation. Even the law, with its inequities and injustices and paganisms, knows better than to let a person sit in judgment of his own case. The answer is the answer of Hosea:

> Their deeds do not permit them,
>   to return to their God.
> For the spirit of harlotry is with them,
>   and they know not the Lord.

For if Hosea is not the answer to why we need to repent but cannot, then the preaching of John and his baptism of Jesus are sentimental and liberal, and relevant to what *we* want (the great "I'm sorry") and not to what *God* demands: "Bear fruits that befit repentance, and do not begin to say to yourselves, 'We have Abraham as our father'; for I tell you, God is able from these stones to raise up children to Abraham" (Lk. 3, 8).

The proclamation of the Gospel is impeded, if not denied, when the demythology and hermeneutic cults demand: "First we must consider the significance of John's world-view and the meaning of language." The heart of repentance is eschatological, apocalyptic: "Even now the axe is laid to the root of the trees; every tree therefore that does not bear good fruit is cut down and thrown into the fire" (Lk. 3, 9).

We must "bear fruits that befit repentance." Let us therefore play with cheap repentance no longer. To gag about cheap repentance is appropriate, but it is insufficient for biblical repentance—the turn, the reversal, the denial of the way we have been going, and the destruction of those barriers of evil deeds that have kept our face from the Lord. Hence, repentance is eschatological, for it does for us what we cannot do for ourselves. "And the multitudes asked him, 'What then shall we do?' And he answered them, 'He who has two coats, let him share with him who has none; and he who has food, let him do likewise'" (Lk. 3, 10-11). John the Baptist knew that this is the very thing we are unable to do. To *be* brother to our brother is what our sins do not permit us to do. We cannot return to God in the radical, either/or quality that John describes as repentance: that we share whatever it is we have with those who have nothing. That is why talk about repentance in the Bible is always shot through with apocalypticism, and has nothing, absolutely nothing, to do with charity or gifts or a world-view that requires demythologizing. Therefore, we should calmly and without fanfare petition God for the gift of repentance which will enable us to do what we cannot do—that is, to share what we have, including the "Good News," with those who have not.

As for our churches, let us calmly and without fanfare petition God for the gift of repentance which will, following John's imagery, incinerate every structure, every institution, every agency, every activity, every seminary, every college, every scheme, every theology, every ambition which pierces anew the body of Christ by denying in word and deed the Good News of Christ's life for all men, which accepts man's inhumanity to man in our incineration of the little children, our brothers and sisters in Christ, in the evil which is about to overwhelm us: racism-war.

Hosea identified the apostasy of the people of Israel as Baalism, that culture-religion which seduced Israel into believing that its "problems" could be met by a religion of nature, by worship at Baal shrines that included the sympathetic magic of "religious" prostitution. This is the heart of Hosea's indictment: "For a spirit of harlotry has led them astray, and they have left their God to play the harlot" (Hos. 4, 12). In spite of God's gifts, mercies and interventions, Israel was governed by the spirit of harlotry, not by the covenant that bound God to them in *hesed,* in steadfast love, as Hosea indicated (9, 10):

> Like grapes in the wilderness,
>   I found Israel.
> Like the first fruit on the fig tree,
>   in its first season,
>   I saw your fathers.
> But they came to Baal-peor.
>   and consecrated themselves to Baal
>   and became detestable like the thing they loved.

For how long now—begin modern politics where you will—has the Church, like Israel, followed the prevailing culture-religion, and been led, like Israel, into a state of apostasy? Instead of the Baal of 8th-century Palestine, we follow politics as our Messiah and accept the *logos* of the political messiah, war. Politics is our Baal, more theologically than analogously. As Baal was the false messiah that led Israel into harlotry and apostasy, to the deeds that did "not permit her to return to God," and hence into God's judgment, so we have accepted modernity's culture-religion that presumes to seal off "this planet earth" and insist that the contradictions between man and man—evil—are exclusively social, thus admitting of *only* political solutions. There is nothing "beyond" this world to which man could be in contradiction, or which could in any way effect that contradiction between man and other men. The scope and reach of politics can admit no limit without threatening the whole faith of modernity. Thus, when political or social intransigence reaches a certain point, and sufficient power—armaments, napalm, financial and economic resources, national guards—is available, it finally "overcomes" by eliminating the bodies of those who persist in their intransigence. President Johnson, following one of the more pacific and rational of our Founding Fathers (Thomas Jefferson), explained this in a State of the Union message: it sometimes becomes necessary to follow a lesser evil in order to prevent a greater one.

Of course it does. God knows, if anything can be learned from personal experience and the study of history, it is that fact. But *that* is not apostasy. The apostasy is that the Church has not only acquiesced in the cult of political Baalism that permits war—the destruction of life for political reasons, life which, as it concerns God, is not our own—to be the final arbiter in the affairs between man and man, *as if there were no other way.* But the Church has also proudly, self-righteously, and in obedience to the world, not the Gospel, proclaimed this as the peculiar if not the only contribution that Christianity can make to the modern world. Since the period of modern politics began sometime in the 15th century, our prayers have called for the total victory of *our* side and the unconditional surrender or else annihilation of the *other side*. We have done this, whether as Church-type, sanctifying the main elements of culture and economics, or the sect-type, sanctifying a dualism of Gospel-and-world which rejects the incarnation and the benefits of Christ's death and resurrection "for all . . . men, while still in life" (2 Cor. 5, 15). Whether in the name of Christian piety, Christian realism, Christian relevance to a world-come-of-age or "the other task of theology," the effect has been the same: we have denied that there was any other way; we have failed to evangelize; we have crucified Christ anew. Thus we have endorsed what the world of modernity already knows (or thinks it knows); we have approved and in some instances tried to sanctify what the world was going to do anyway, however reluctantly and with or without our support.

Is it any wonder that our testimony on racism-war—in the face of the chilling awareness that America is racist and the tragic witness of Vietnam—is not credible? Is it any wonder that the witness of the Church to the world is taken seriously by so very, very few, regardless of how desperately we insist that we *are* credible, that we *are* serious, that our message *is* relevant, secular, humane, and all the rest? We have participated in and actively supported the illusion that is beginning to prove fatal to the modern world—that politics is redemptive, that what cannot be cured by peaceful political action must be secured by a dramatic, albeit reluctant, extension of political action into the destruction of the bodies of "the other side," of those who are determined not to let us have our "way." In short, we have rejected *the one witness* that would have made the Church credible in the very "modern world" we now seek so desperately and so pathologically to "celebrate." We rejected the one Word, the only Word, we could have proclaimed and confessed that somehow might have diluted the acids which have so corroded our world. We failed to witness against the Baalism of modern politics; we failed to proclaim that politics was not redemptive. Instead, we followed the spirit of harlotry of the culture-religion of our age; we accepted politics as the Messiah. It is always the Church, not the world, which crucifies Christ anew.

Let us be clear: we are no more talking about eliminating or rejecting "politics" in the face of the Church's apostasy about politics-as-Baal than the Bible is talking about rejecting "sex" because of Baal religious prostitution. Neither course is possible. Barth's aphorism about philosophy is equally applicable to politics: when we open our mouths, we are in the realm of "politics," much as to live as a human is to live "sexually" and philosophically, and the denial thereof merely proves the fact. Politics, as a minimum, is the means whereby we organize relatively, externally and provisionally the relations between and among men—so that what Aristotle said about man being a "political animal" is, to that extent, true. In that sense, "politics" is all that man "has"—or, speaking theologically, is what God has given man—to organize himself in greater and smaller communities, in order to extend the requirements of justice as *right* relations between and among men. But these are *relative, external* and *provisional* relationships that are the concern of the activities and institutions of politics. They are not Messiah, nor can they be made Messiah; they cannot redeem fallen man, and to engage in politics as redemptive is idolatry, Baalism. This is the seduction that defines the fate of the modern world, the same seduction that drags us into the age of technology, the technopolis, the age when we can least afford this particular idol. The apostasy of the Church is its failure and unwillingness to witness against this idolatry, and worse, to accept and follow this seduction.

The complicity of the Church is all the more tragic when one considers the current efforts to define *"post*-Christendom" and "secularism" as recent phenomena, and to reflect upon the periodic revivals of religious interests in the West, especially the United States, which invariably cite more people attending church services, more interest in religion among college students, more young people entering religious service, more money spent (or invested) by religious agencies, etc.—the criteria of modernity. Hosea was not unfamiliar with this sort of business. Consider this analysis and indictment against the priests of his day (4, 7-10):

> The more they increased,
>   the more they sinned against me;
>   I will change their glory into shame.
> They feed on the sin of my people;
>   they are greedy for their iniquity.
> And it shall be like people, like priest;
>   I will punish them for their ways,
>   and requite them for their deeds.
> They shall eat, but not be satisfied;
>   they shall play the harlot, but not multiply;
> because they have forsaken the Lord
>   to cherish harlotry.

The axe has been and is being laid to the root of much of the present decay and petrifaction in the institutional Church, and has been and is being cut down before our eyes and cast into the fire. So long as we cling to these empty and rotten shells, our deeds will not permit us to return to God, since we will not be able to "bear fruits that befit repentance." For, indeed, such structures and institutions are indistinguishable from those outside the Church (the political institutions and structures of politics-as-Baal) that are likewise being cast into the fire by their incapacity and inability to meet the political demands of the last third of the 20th century.

The dilemma of modernity and the apostasy of the Church are not resolved by anarchy—in trying to abjure political responsibility by casting politics as the one devil responsible for everything that ails us—any more than politics-as-Baal can redeem us. The time may be upon us when certain forms of political action, dear to those who glory in our 18th-century traditions, will have to be rejected—perhaps temporarily, perhaps permanently—in order to topple idols and thereby refocus upon political reality. Public education as a guarantor of democracy is one. Presidential politics and elections are another, and easier, example. Moreover, no more law is needed to have a go at presidential politics—at least at the moment of writing. In any event, avowed refusal to participate in presidential elections (something not "tolerated" in regimes which we have been told are hostile to the "free world") would do more to shift attention to the political reality of the 20th century than a dozen blue-ribbon, silk-stocking panels of distinguished citizens and a hundred inquiries by political scientists. For the truth is that at the present time voting in presidential elections is a gesture of futility, a form, a feint on the part of the two-party consensus, and it has been that since the 1930's in this country, if not earlier. Political scientists might well correlate the hysterical reaction in the Establishment (including the Church) to low voter-turnouts and registration programs (especially among certain "minorities") to the pride in high voter-turnout by the regimes which* we have been told are hostile to the "free world." Avowed refusal to participate in presidential politics would be an important political witness against the idolatry of *democracy-by-elections,* against the fiction that democracy is identical with the two-party system, against the patent contradiction to democracy found in presidential politics. To be sure, it would bring wails of "Anarchy!" and "Defeatism!" from those locked in the liberal illusions of the politics-equals-elections-equals-two-party-system. But that would be the proof of just how *political* the action was.

Some wonder about Elijah, Amos, Jeremiah, Jesus and Paul today: Would they smoke pot and wear sandals, or drink bourbon and wear cowboy boots? We wonder about them today also. We wonder about them . . . voting! We wonder about them getting up-tight and forming discussion groups around Theodore White's various books on *The Making of the President* in order to make a rational choice *for* . . . Nixon-Agnew or Humphrey-Muskie or Wallace-Lemay or Lindsay-Kennedy or . . . ?

And then we wonder about the Berrigans.

It is our worship of politics—not politics itself or our participation in politics—that is the Baal which must be toppled. We do well to remind ourselves that the Hebrew prophets, although they held Nazarites and Rechabites in some esteem, were never tempted to join these movements which, among other things, rejected the very fact of Israel's political life in Canaan. Nor did these prophets—in spite of the ambiguous tradition concerning the establishment of the Hebrew monarchy—counsel kings to abdicate and people to reject political responsibility because it was *political.* It was in political activity that one's obedience to the terms of the covenant could be made explicit and obvious. And that is the point that needs to be emphasized. Politics-as-Baal is seduction by the worship of political activity as such. Politics-as-Baal is to act in the belief that politics is redemptive, that politics is Messiah —as if one more civil rights bill, one more two-year grant of money against poverty, one more stance against "communism" at the "invitation" of despotic and inhuman political regimes, one more intervention by what President Eisenhower called the "military-industrial (and, we must add, 'technological') complex," one more escalation, will do it, and then the Kingdom of God, the Great Society, Scientific Humanism will be here. This will *never* happen because it *can* never happen. God knows that there is much wrong with us politically, socially and economically, and that is what political activity should make its order of business—those external, relative, provisional arrangements which deal with social and economic and political inequities and injustices. Nevertheless, we must understand from the outset that those ailments which are political and can be cured by politics *will not* be cured so long as we persist in the illusion that politics can cure *everything* that is wrong with us. What is wrong with us that can be solved by politics is not all that is wrong with us. But so long as we indulge in the illusion—specifically, for us, so long as the Church follows politics-as-Baal—that there are no limits to what politics can solve and ought to solve, politics is bound to fail us, to lead the disillusioned persecuted and persecutor to stand and glare and threaten and in the end know only how to destroy the "other" who refused to be subjected to another's political solution.

If politics is means, not Messiah, if there are ills we suffer that cannot be diagnosed as exclusively social or political or economic, if there is something wrong between and among men that technology, laws and money can neither touch nor remedy, to whom shall we go? In our view, to ask the question, at least in that manner, is to answer it. "Peter replied for himself and the apostles: 'We must obey God rather than men. The God of our fathers raised up Jesus whom you had put to death by hanging him on a gibbet. He it is whom God has exalted with his own right hand as leader and savior, to grant Israel repentance and forgiveness of sins. And we are witnesses to all this, and so is the Holy Spirit given by God to those who are obedient to him' " (Acts 5, 30-32).

The particular relevance of this overquoted passage is that it is the sum of what we have been trying to say about "repentance and politics." Peter speaks for us as well as "for himself and the apostles" when he says that "we must obey God rather than men," for, lest we forget, these words are directed to religious authorities, *not* political authorities. The People of God, as the prophets and apostles knew so well, do not exist to shake angry fists or thrust relevant socio-political data at the "world," and especially the political world, shouting, "Repent! Repent!" Repentance has no meaning outside "Israel." Our relation to the world is not to threaten and warn, but to serve. This means that we cannot serve the world by trying to prescribe the very poison that daily hastens its death, the faith in politics-as-Messiah. By serving—without fanfare, with no questions asked, whenever and wherever persons are sovereign over principle and institution and ideologies—the Church *is* related to the world as Christ is related to the world: this way, and no other, because in this way, and no other, Jesus Christ was related to the world.

As for us, our faith in Christ as Messiah forms the basis for repentance which we—not the "world"—must undergo for having served the Baalism of modern politics. Let those who sneer at John Calvin's "authoritarianism" consider this: "We are subject to the men who rule over us, but subject only in the Lord. If they command anything against him, let us not pay the least regard to it, nor be moved by all the dignity which they possess as magistrates—a dignity to which no injury is done when it is subordinated to the special and truly supreme power of God. . . . And that our courage may not fail, Paul stimulates us by the additional consideration (1 Cor. 7, 23) that we were redeemed by Christ at the great price which our redemption cost him, in order that we might not yield a slavish obedience to the depraved wishes of men, far less do homage to their impiety" (*Institutes* IV, 20, 32).

Finally, let us remember the admonition of John 15, 20, "A servant is not greater than his master," as well as the words of Luke 4, 5-8:

Next the devil led him up and showed him in a flash all the kingdoms of the world. "All this dominion will I give

Politics as Baal 73

you," he said, "and the glory that goes with it; for it has been put in my hand and I can give it to anyone I choose. You have only to do homage to me and it shall be yours." Jesus answered him, "Scripture says, 'You shall do homage to the Lord your God and worship him alone.' "

VII
The Paradigm of Dixie Hills

In June 1967 we witnessed the occupation of Dixie Hills by the police in Atlanta, Georgia. It was an efficient operation, within ten minutes sealing black citizens off from their streets and from their treeless and grassless yards, and into the oppressive summer heat of their sweltering apartment buildings whose windows defy air-conditioning. But the meaning of this efficiency—one might say, the rationality of the operation—cannot obscure the irrationality, the meaninglessness of the occupation of Dixie Hills. What problems were solved, what issues met, by the police driving black citizens from their streets and yards and doorways? A "riot"? "Gun battles between police and Negroes" (as one wire service reported)? There were none at the time the police were there, and the best evidence is that none were threatened. "Protection of human life?" A 49-year-old resident was killed and a 9-year-old child critically wounded—struck down in the doorway of one of the apartment buildings by what were apparently two blasts of buckshot—less than half an hour after the police had "cleared" the troubled area.

Dixie Hills is a paradigm for the new South, if not the whole of America, for it prefigures what happens and is going to happen when law, with its occupation and pacification by shotguns and carbines, is the only answer that a technically efficient modern police force can give when faced with what it determines—and political leaders are powerless to reject —as "racially troubled areas."

There had been, in the canned phrase of radio reports, "intermittent trouble" in the area for two days. Dixie Hills is made up in part of the sort of modest and near middle-class homes in black ghettos that are the pride of the liberal politician, businessman, church and civic leader and newspaper editor, North or South—a pride that causes them to wring their hands and cry in disbelief when "racial" trouble occurs, "But this is *not* a slum area!" The "trouble," however, was not in the area of these homes. It was confined to the part of Dixie Hills that encompasses a large apartment building complex. In this area there is some black—as well as the customary white—ownership and management. These apartments were once a less than satisfactory domicile for middle-class black Atlantans. But as the areas of black occupancy of better housing have increased, the apartments have become largely occupied by poorer black working-class people and welfare recipients, and their number includes people relocated from slums destroyed by urban renewal. There is much overcrowding of the small hot units.

There is a shopping center of four or five buildings which include the West Side Neighborhood Service Center. The Service Center is a Poverty Program project which channels jobs, youth activities, educational opportunities and social services to the residents of the area. Surrounding the shopping center on three sides are rows of two-story low-rent apartment buildings—not unlike brick army barracks on the outside—privately owned and noted for their capacity to retain the summer heat of Georgia, even long after nightfall. They have been described as "unbearable" in the daytime. There are no recreation facilities in the area—no swimming pools, playgrounds, parks or movies, private or otherwise. One of the activities of the Neighborhood Service Center is to bus youngsters across to the Butler Street YMCA, and the workers at the Center were planning for the next day's busing during the time of the Dixie Hills disturbances. Complaints about the refusal of the apartment owners to spray properly for roaches and rats, about inadequate garbage collection, about poor recreation facilities and especially about the lack of jobs—these had been in the air for months.

To the case in point: On the Sunday preceding the trouble at Dixie Hills on Tuesday, Stokely Carmichael had been arrested at the shopping center for refusing to obey the orders of the Atlanta police to "go on." There was no riot at the time, and evidence suggests that he was not making "militant" and "threatening" speeches in the name of "Black Power." Mr. Carmichael said (under oath) at the subsequent trial that he and two other SNCC workers had been swimming and had driven by the shopping center to drop off two children who were riding home with them and to check on one or two residents in the area who had been arrested a few days before. The police said that they had received a call from Dixie Hills reporting that Carmichael was in the area, trying to start trouble. One of the arresting officers testified that "when we arrived we found a goodly crowd at the shopping center." Five minutes later, the officer continued, Carmichael spoke to a Negro policeman and then walked over toward "our car," asking "Man, what you got all these police cars here for? The first thing you know, we'll have a riot here." The officer testified that he told Carmichael: "This is a troubled area. You do not live in this area and I suggest you go on." According to the officer, Carmichael replied, "Man, don't tell me where I live." He was arrested when he refused to "go on." At the trial, Carmichael explained that he "had stopped to talk to some girls about wearing their hair natural and being proud of being black because they are beautiful," and that, continuing to his car, he saw "ten or twelve squad cars pull up" around the parking lot at the shopping center.

Carmichael and his two companions spent the night in jail, and on Monday they returned to Dixie Hills and the shopping center for a "press conference." Shortly after the conference broke up, a young married resident of Dixie Hills was shot in the leg by a policeman near the grocery store of the shopping center in an incident that is still confused but which reportedly had something to do with a burglar alarm. One report said that the victim had not attended the SNCC news conference at the shopping center. Early that same evening, residents and leaders held a meeting to present complaints and to plan for action. From the account of newsmen who were present, Carmichael and other SNCC leaders spoke, defiantly and militantly. Carmichael's performance was, for him, restrained. He told the audience to "cool it" until police left the area. Between such warnings, however, he talked an angry, "Black Power" line, and as the meeting was breaking up, someone shouted, "Remember Watts. Burn, baby, burn." Subsequently, some serious rock throwing occurred after dark in the area of the shopping center, injuring two policemen and two newsmen. Eleven blacks were arrested.

On Tuesday, SNCC workers, including the new national chairman, H. Rap Brown, and Willie Ricks, were in the area, opposing a "leadership" plan to organize anti-riot youth patrols. And they were saying what everybody expects them to say: that "we're going to make Vietnam look like a holiday," that after 8 o'clock, no more "cops and white folks" would be allowed in Dixie Hills, that they were going "to blow up" the situation in the area, and that this was "just a prelude to what America is in for." Yet it seemed clear that the residents did not take this too seriously, and some of the white reporters joked about being able to leave at 8:00 P.M. Indeed, the SNCC folk would appear to have evoked less attention from the residents than did the police, who must now be (along with the rest of America) prisoners of their self-fulfilling conviction that "wherever Stokely goes" trouble and riots will follow. At any event, on the evening that the police occupied Dixie Hills, the residents, as one newsman said, "were more curious than hostile."

During the long, daylight-saving-time evening, the people of Dixie Hills had eaten dinner, and instead of sweltering before the TV inside their oven-hot living quarters, they decided on the obvious—to go outside, out of the ovens, and watch what was happening in the shopping center across the street. Some of them rested on the fenders of their automobiles, or gathered in small groups in their baked, red-clay yards, or sat on the curbs or on the steps of the apartment buildings. There was plenty to watch. The mass media had been gathered for a couple of days, primed, perhaps even hopeful, for a good session of visible news. Joseph Boone of SCLC and Leroy Johnson, the first Negro state senator in Georgia since Reconstruction ("their" Senator), had also been talking, organizing meetings and youth patrols for a day or two—that is, since Carmichael's appearance on Sunday. Everyone was wondering: "Is Stokely coming back?" The TV and radio station wagons and their crews had been in the parking area in front of the shopping center for most of the afternoon, although a soft drink distributor had refused all day to enter the area and replenish the supply of his goods in the depleted machine located in the rear of the Neighborhood Service Center building. There were also a few black and white patrolmen and police officers and a dozen black and white newsmen and radio reporters. To the residents of Dixie Hills, who were "more curious than hostile," this far outdid the lazy reruns on the TV gleaming inside the buildings and adding to the heat. Anyway, this was the first time that so much attention had been paid to them.

As if on a signal some rocks were thrown. No one was hurt; perhaps one or two windows were broken. The TV crews went into action, the fetus-camera straining the umbilical cords on the battery boxes, up and down the parking lot. Some TV crewmen and newsmen strapped on what looked like World War II helmet-liners. The signal thrown by the arrest of three or four blacks called in the patrol cars which had been poised on the outskirts of the shopping center. Within ten minutes, the shopping center and the apartment houses were occupied by the racially integrated police force. Armed with shotguns and wearing blue riot helmets, they cleared the area by forcing residents back into their steaming apartment buildings. The patrol that remained was manned by Negro and white policemen on foot, and cars with Negro and white officers threw the intimidating spotlight into the channels between the barracks-like apartment buildings and on any suspicious sound, object, gathering or individual. Residents returning to the area on foot or in their cars were escorted by the police to their apartment buildings, as if into the "administrative concentration camps" one hears about from an occasional sociologist.

A few minutes later—not more than ten or fifteen—sharp sounds could be heard, but no one was sure whether they (or which ones) were gunshots or firecrackers until a red ambulance of Grady Hospital roared up and stopped in front of the apartment barracks at 31 Shirley Place. They carried away the stilled bodies of a young boy and a middle-aged man. When the shock of the meaningless terror of seeing a companion and a child cut down in a matter of seconds had given way to reflection and recrimination, those who had been sitting on the front steps of 31 Shirley Place with the victims confirmed each other's account. They had rushed for the inside of the building through a door leading to the first floor apartments and to the stairway to the second floor as soon as they saw a Molotov cocktail explode in the street near the patrolmen. Some insisted that they had seen a patrolman fire directly at them after the explosion. One said bitterly that when the residents shouted to the policemen who were in the street that wounded people were on the landing at the end of the concrete steps, they had shouted back from the street, "Bring them out here!" The young man who had been shot by the police the day before in the shopping center, and had that afternoon volunteered for the youth anti-riot patrol, gave a statement to black leaders (and to a black newsman who put it on a tape recording), charging that the police had fired the fatal shot. But the officers directing the occupation of Dixie Hills insisted that no patrolmen were in the vicinity where the fatal blast had been discharged. It *had* to be a sniper, they said. (But we heard no one volunteer an explanation of why "a sniper"— presumably a black—would have fired at other blacks fleeing from the explosion of a Molotov cocktail.) The patrolmen said that no matter how clearly "we" prove that "we" didn't do it, "they'll" insist that "we" did. One of the men who had been patrolling the area of 31 Shirley Place anticipated a liedetector test and said that they could check his shotgun to prove that it had not been fired.

So it went. Those who had known the victim and had shared his last moments on this earth moaned about how he was just trying to get out of "their" way after the fire-bomb had exploded in the street, about how he had been so cautious about the "trouble" centering on the shopping center, that he had that very afternoon refused to go to the shopping center for a loaf of bread. They insisted that they had not been expecting "trouble" that night—else why would they have been sitting on their front steps with children and women around? Responding to white reporters, they asked, "How would *you* feel if, on returning home from work and eating dinner, you had seen a companion killed who minutes before had been sitting beside you talking to you, and you had stretched out a child in your living room, wounded by a gunshot—for reasons that make no sense, for events that had nothing to do with you?"

The policemen talked freely with, indeed sought out, newsmen to explain what had and was happening. One officer made the point that it was never those who "deserved" killing who always seemed to be the victims in such situations; then he began a series of disclaimers to the effect that "no one deserved killing, of course," serving only to emphasize rather than mitigate his initial statement. The youth of the patrolmen on the front line of the occupation was striking. We do not recall seeing any who looked older than twenty-five. Black and white, they were uneasy and rightly saw themselves as the enemy of the residents of the occupied territory. Their relation to their superior officers seemed vague. One wondered how many had been in the armed services because of Vietnam, and were still within that span of years so dearly beloved by the military since the beginning of organized armies.

One cannot help but noting the parallel between the white-hooded klansmen in the backcountry and the blue-helmeted patrolmen in Dixie Hills. What separated the two groups, beyond years, and geography, and the prose of Faulkner or Warren? In both instances, force was used to seal human beings into the darkened corners of all that passed for black "homes" in a white land. In both instances, a meaninglessness, a caprice, hovered, that translated itself into a hopelessness, an acceptance of fate—with only an occasional exception to be found in the eyes of young blacks. In both instances, the uniform gave a kind of sanction, if not a legality, to terrorize and intimidate those whose only crime seemed to be the color of the skin of their forebears who were stolen in the manner of animals from their home on another continent by men of another color—except that in Dixie Hills, the blue-helmets of the riot squad cancelled out the blackness of the patrolmen's skin, so long as they kept the blue helmets on and remained in Dixie Hills. Perhaps what finally separates the white hoods from the blue helmets is time and technology. Perhaps this is part of what it means for "the world to come of age." Is not the difference between the legality of the blue helmets and the paralegality of the white hoods diminished by the irrational rationality, the impersonal, the technical efficiency of police occupation of "troubled racial areas" that—like the irrational rationality of the bombs over Coventry and Hiroshima and Vietnam—by definition cannot make the distinctions between innocent individuals and "troubled areas"? Does not the Gospel's account of Herod's slaughter of the innocents "make sense" in a world come of age?

The night Dixie Hills was occupied by the integrated police force of Atlanta was the night that "the new South" was given a paradigm of racism in a region advancing mightily in trade, industry and technology, a region which uses and is used by a technologically efficient and therefore racially integrated police force. It was the night, following earlier nights in Jackson, Mississippi, and Houston, Texas, that "the new South" joined the efficiency in these matters of most of the rest of the nation. Innocence or guilt of specific individuals regarding a specific law is of secondary consequence to the efficient clearing and pacification of a "racially troubled area." One of the slain man's friends said that it really didn't make

The Paradigm of Dixie Hills

much difference who had killed him: "He's dead, that's all." And he was right. That *is* the point.

A well-known Southern journalist and advocate of New South liberalism wrote about the events that Tuesday evening in Dixie Hills in his syndicated column in the *Atlanta Constitution*. The title of the column was "Charlatans: Black— White." It began: "It was after I read that death and property destruction had come to a Negro community from violence incited by SNCC field worker Stokely Carmichael that I found myself thinking of the more successful white charlatans of the past—and present." He noted the irony, "perhaps an inevitable one, that a Negro organization should emerge which is a black Ku Klux Klan following the white Klan that flourished during the 1920's." He referred darkly to SNCC's "plan of violence," to its weapons of "coercion and fear," its "inner secret organization for violence," and to the fact that it "operated now on cash, having attained a bad credit rating," which "cash . . . is funneled into New York and disbursed chiefly through three individuals. Sources of the cash are also known." He named neither those who disbursed the "cash," nor the "sources of the cash." More importantly, he failed to explain what *his* readers of all readers needed most desperately to understand: that the Klan of the 1920's was in many respects an adjunct of the predominant political and economic structure of the South, whereas SNCC can hardly be called an adjunct of anything predominant in the United States, and that it proposes to speak and act not for anything dominant, but precisely for those oppressed by what is dominant in the United States, black and/or white. It is one thing to entertain grave misgivings about the white-like militancy of some SNCC statements ("We're going to make Vietnam look like a holiday"). But that is not really important. That is not the issue. What must be said—clearly and without equivocation—is that the failure to recognize this critical distinction between the Klan of the 1920's and the SNCC of the 1960's is already proving costly. The cost is the reality and the increasing hopelessness and desperation of impoverished and dispossessed blacks in the urban ghettos and in the backcountry, the increased militancy of

SNCC, the predictable increase of (in the journalist's phrase) "death and property destruction," and the erosion of the soul of the white Southerner—especially the liberal white Southerner.

On the Monday before the Tuesday that Dixie Hills was occupied, the Atlanta Board of Aldermen passed an ordinance conferring powers on the mayor to deal with "emergency situations," including the use of city employees other than the police to preserve order and protect property, and the right to close off streets and sidewalks, business establishments and municipally owned buildings and other facilities. Ivan Allen of Atlanta epitomizes the increasing helplessness of mayors to deal with any degree of hope in the "racially troubled areas" of American ghettos. He toured Dixie Hills the night the police occupied it, returned to City Hall, signed a proclamation declaring an emergency, and invoked a dusk-to-dawn curfew for residents of the area. It was not clear from the proclamation what the residents of Dixie Hills had done to deserve the curfew. But Mayor Allen is as helpless before the demands of "responsible" citizens on the one hand and the technical apparatus of his police force on the other, as, say, the President of the United States and the Premier of Russia are before their constituents and their industrial-military complexes—once the only decision is made that the world of the 20th century seems to be willing, eager, and able to make to solve its political problems: the force of arms (in this instance, to clear, occupy and pacify "racially troubled areas"). It matters little that black leaders prevailed upon the mayor to lift the curfew before it had a chance to go into effect, or that the first black state senator in Georgia since Reconstruction was obtaining upward of 1,000 signatures from residents of Dixie Hills asking "those persons who had caused or aided in causing turmoil in our community to leave and let the residents of this area restore peace in our community." Nor did it really matter that the bulk of the occupation force left the area within twelve hours.

The Paradigm of Dixie Hills

If one wants to know what Dixie Hills means, he should ponder the question: Does not the mere possibility of racial violence in America today protect, indeed exacerbate, the very forces creating the danger which may very well destroy what remains of our democracy? If the answer is "Yes," police occupation of what the political order defines as "racially troubled areas" cannot overcome, but in fact enhances, the threat that bids fair to bring an end to what remains of democracy in America—a danger inextricably related to international politics conducted under the shadow of atomic apocalypse, but one that will nonetheless persist if the shadow should somehow miraculously lift. The threat feeds on itself. For centuries our society has seduced itself into believing that any threat to law and order can be eliminated by the use of armed force. Such a belief in the efficacy of force heightens the threat because, in its efficiency, police power in the technological society, if it is to serve properly the dominant political order, must become impersonal, indiscriminate and thereby an enemy of justice. (Such a belief, incidentally, will gradually yet inevitably corrode the law itself, as can already be seen in the inability of legal authorities to cope with the dilemma posed by the *illegal* use of drugs by young people and the *legal* use of alcohol by older people, as well as with the demand for political freedom and economic justice by black people and the demand for political order and the protection of property and its values by white people.) Hence the threat cannot be isolated to "racially troubled areas," or even to the existence of ghettos or to political, economic and social discrimination. These are merely symptoms, expressions. One might call the threat "racism." But racism in America today is really an expression of who we are as a people, of the state of our commonwealth, of our perverted sense of values, of our idolatry of force and of the material and sensate, and of the political messianism that lurks in all the nostrums we brandish at one another.

In Dixie Hills, as in Watts, Houston and the rest, the justice of police action is a matter of secondary consequence. What does matter is that the "troubled area" is successfully secured by efficient police action, which efficiency and action have become a law and order unto themselves. Dixie Hills reveals that, to use Walter Lippmann's phrase, America is sick, not wounded. It reveals the extent of our sickness in our refusal to take heed of what is happening to us, for we refuse to acknowledge that we are ill. It reveals no signs—either in the major political parties and their Birchite or ADA satellites, or in the alleged "new politics"— pointing out a way to meet the threat without exacerbating it. As William Faulkner said: "If we in America have reached that point in our desperate culture when we must murder children, no matter for what reason or what color, we don't deserve to survive, and probably won't."

VIII
If We Should Get Serious

Much was said about the past few summers. Much had been predicted about them.

Little which had been predicted actually came to pass. Each time we were spared. Each time the patience of black Americans endured. To be sure there have been a few uprisings—but only a few—with a dozen or so cities each year experiencing a murmur of discontent. In the whole of American society such murmurs seemed little more than a rustle of thought, heard by an unheeding few. A dozen or so cities a year. But America has 678 cities. Several dozen people were killed, mostly black people—children, men and old women. White America shrugged it off as too bad, but something which had to be done.

At a recent meeting of a department of Christian social relations of a large Protestant denomination, it was reported that 3,800 50-caliber bullet holes were found in one Detroit wall where an elderly grandmother was killed. It was further reported that a 50-caliber machine gun bullet will pierce twelve inches of armor. Rising to the defense of the National Guard, a Midwestern minister of Jesus Christ sought to "keep the record straight." "A 50-caliber machine gun bullet will not pierce twelve inches of armor," he protested. "It will only pierce two inches of armor and then only if it is fired straight in." Never mind the children's Granny. Let's keep the record straight.

It is interesting that each year we are once again spared. Not yet does the dream deferred fester like a sore, stink like rotten meat, or crust over. And not yet has it exploded as Langston Hughes predicted it would. Who would have thought it? Who would have dreamed that by now we would not be saying, as our Lord said we would say, "Blessed are the barren, and the wombs that never bore, and the paps which never gave suck"; ". . . to the mountains, 'Fall on us'; and to the hills, 'Cover us.' " From the predictions made prior to each summer's advent we would have thought that by now our destruction would have been so great as to cause us to cry out that it was more tolerable for Tyre and Sidon on their day of judgment than for us on our day of judgment.

But it did not happen. Only a dozen or so cities each year felt the murmur. And they killed some and jailed some and now go on.

But what of the rest of us? What of the 678 cities? Is there yet time? Will we escape the judgment? Can we yet be saved? Did we hear anything? Wretched men that we are, who will deliver us?

Because we escape one summer does not mean we will escape the next summer and the next. And the summers seem destined now to stretch into winter and spring. Only God knows if we will be spared. He has been known to destroy the righteous with the wicked, the victors with the vanquished, but he has also been known to promise to spare a wicked generation if fifty, forty-five, forty, thirty, twenty, or ten righteous ones could be found. Perhaps the uprisings of the last few summers were a warning, with God saying to us: "Because the cry of Sodom and Gomorrah is great, and because their sin is very grievous, I will go down now, and see whether they have done altogether according to the outcry which has come unto me; and if not, I will know." If so, we have already done as those standing before God with Abraham who "turned their faces from thence, and went toward Sodom." But Abraham stood yet before the Lord. Who in our day will stand toe to toe with God and plead that the wicked be spared with the righteous?

Will the Church?

If We Should Get Serious 89

We have in the past said that it is too late for the Church to "do something" in the racial crisis. It may well be that it is too late for us to escape the wrath, the awful day of judgment, the burning cities, the 3,800 50-caliber holes in one wall. But it is never too late for faithfulness. And that is our only vocation.

How can the Church stand before God now and plead: "If perchance there are fifty righteous men within the city, will you also destroy and not spare the place for the fifty righteous that are therein?"

How? We have also in the past said some very mean and hard things about the institutional Church. Enough of that! To stand and damn the past sins of the Church can no longer be considered an act of faithfulness. We who curse it the loudest are often those who served and worshiped it the longest. We should have known better than to worship it and to see it as anything more than a tool which could either wear out or, as in our case, rust out. To curse it now is like paying to go to bed with a whore and then going into a rage at the discovery that she is not a virgin. We should have known.

Repentance is concerned with the future. And what of the future? What possible acts of faithfulness are left?

Our holy marches on Washington and Selma, our certified U.N. observers, our admonitions to the White House and our mandates to Capitol Hill are Babel now. Maybe they were such from the beginning. What then is left to us? How may we witness to the Gospel in the face of judgment?

We might begin by bringing back to our shores the 29,000 missionaries who are now overseas, putting them to work in the urban and rural crises. But if we do this, let it not be done as a gimmick to cure the crises. (We have had plenty of cures already. The problem was not one of medication but of diagnosis.) Let them be brought back in the name and for the sake of evangelism, the perpetuation of the Christian faith. Let it be done because we at last recognize that there are no heathens left who haven't heard the news of who we are. Let us by so doing admit to those we would win to Christ and his kingdom that we are no fit subjects—that we, after having preached to others, have missed the way ourselves. The sins of America are so grievous, the result of so mishearing the liberating Gospel of Jesus Christ, that we dare not tell it to others any longer lest we succeed in converting them to what we are. But do not bring them back alone. Bring with each one a native saint who has been visited by the Holy Spirit. Let him tell us what we do as against what we preach. Let him come from Vietnam, both South and North, and from Africa and South America. Let him tell of the napalm and the sudden smell of burning flesh, of the famines, the wars and plagues, the starvation—*not in his land but in ours.* And let him give us a fresh look at what the Good News really is.

Let them be Parthians, and Medes, and Elamites, and the dwellers in Mesopotamia and in Judea, and Cappadocia, in Pontus and Asia, Phrygia, and Pamphylia, in Egypt, and in the parts of Libya about Cyrene, and strangers of Rome, Jews and proselytes, Cretes and Arabians, and perhaps the Church can be born again, even if among the ruins and ashes of our cities.

IX
Violence and Snopes

Detroit, Newark, Milwaukee, Washington—cities afire, cities simmering, while others have been spared. Is it too hasty or unduly pessimistic to offer the judgment that once again we have learned *nothing?*

Have we learned nothing because we have passed the point when we can be made to know in our hearts that something is dreadfully, perhaps fatally, wrong with us? Do our sins "not permit us to return to God?" (Hos. 5, 4).

Without exception we react to our civil warfare by reflexes, with hollow gestures. A commission is appointed whose color and composition suggest a magisterial and cynical thumb of the nose by our highest elected official. With strained grief the Chief Executive of "the most powerful nation in history" spends $2 billion a month to save freedom in Asia by killing the Asians. With the same gesture, he commissions a jury, of blue ribbons and silk stockings, to exchange views on the fate of the victims of three hundred years of violence and racism. A visit and a two-hour talk *to any black* in the ghettos of the capital of "the most powerful nation in history," or in East Harlem, Newark or Detroit, or in the 'cropper's cabins in south Alabama or Georgia or the Mississippi or Louisiana Delta would have told him all anyone needed to know. And the Congress of this "most powerful nation in history," with few demurrers, shares this sense of value, priority and political judgment.

And so does the nation. Speeches and editorials and cocktail lounge chatter call for more imaginative use of (or outright abolition of—there is really little difference in the two viewpoints) the Job Corps, the Poverty Program, Black Militancy, riot police and the National Guard, the Black Panthers, Sargeant Shriver, tear gas, Teddy Kennedy, Spiro Agnew, and H. Rap Brown. It is all as cut-and-dried and now as much a part of our system as the war bulletins from Saigon or a statement by the President or Secretary of State or General Westmoreland or General Abrams or Tom Hayden on American aims in Southeast Asia.

This reflex response that is now built into our domestic war front should convince even the most determined optimist that government and politics are unable of themselves to reverse the direction of this nation's racism. Indeed, the contrary is true: our government and politics have for the most part aggravated racism since 1789 or 1865. To say—as do the political theorists of the death of God and the mainline sentiment of the New Politics and the ADA—that "if politics cannot solve our problems then they will not be solved" is simply to state the case and the depth of our tragedy. The sentiment does not change the realities about the direction in which politics and government are taking American racism.

Let us be clear about where we are, and about how we got here. From the very beginning, political involvement in America's racism—national, state, local, Republican, Democrat, Whatnot—when it has not been the instrumentality to preserve white superiority, has, without exception, been skittish, giving half-hearted responses to the revolts and explosions of the black community. Politics has involved itself in American racism *not* because of a sense of injustice, but because blacks reacted with increasing vigor against the miserable and hopeless lot into which America's democracy had cast them. Black indignation and revolt against the politics of American democracy provoked whatever interest politics and government have devoted to ameliorating the most horrifying features of America's racism. Not a sense of injustice, but a sense of frustration, has been the characteristic attitude of American politics toward racial misery and unrest. It was inevitable, therefore, that political frustration would lead us to these present days of blasphemy.

There is, therefore, no sign, no hint—anywhere—that government and politics are capable of redirecting our national life in a way that can end, or even significantly modify, white racism. Government and politics in the 20th century have become dominated by (and therefore obsessed with) the exercise of armed power to meet all problems that seem to threaten the existing social order. Two *world* wars, the increasing ratio of non-combatant deaths from 1914-1918 to Korea and Vietnam, the hydrogen and napalm apocalypse, Sheriffs Clark and Rainey, the riot police and National Guard, and the 3,800 50-caliber holes in one wall in Detroit are the case in point. Government and politics have become the exercise of those instrumentalities that delude themselves and their citizenry into thinking that they can solve political and social crises by destroying the bodies of their political and social opponents. Other functions—social security, health insurance, employment, education, etc.—now devolve from this function. Check any budget of the United States of America since 1940. List those political and social crises that have been "solved"—in the sense of eliminated—by the use of physical force.

Consequently, the most legitimate action government and politics could exercise against racism in America would be self-restraint, a limitation of their own use of physical coercion. But if they did so—we will ask and be asked—how can government be "responsible"? How can it meet its commitments and honor its pledges of law and order here and abroad? How can our shops and streets and investments be made safe if politics and government restrain rather than escalate their use of force? No right-thinking citizen can demand the restraint of the police and National Guard, or ask General Abrams to tie his hands in Southeast Asia. Of course not. The whole direction of our government and politics through the escalation of force in social crises aggravates the situation it seeks to overcome. Democrat, Republican, New Politics and Birchite are simply four identical ways of looking at the same blackbird.

In a word, the violence employed by government and politics to meet the crises of white racism in America incites counterviolence in the victims of this violence. This antiphony of violence by political authority and counterviolence by oppressed blacks, which describes the present state of racism in America today, bids fair to become the obsession that may divert the nation from whatever chance there remains to amend this racism. There is, for example, some evidence suggesting that the study of violence and its "morality" is the next detour that the intellectuals and the theologians will travel. Insofar as Christians are concerned, it is necessary to recall our own witness to and about violence. By and large, since the 3rd century, we have celebrated it, made a cult of it, because we Christians have exercised the preponderance of such violence in Western culture. But when violence occasionally threatens our property (and incidentally our lives) we condemn it—in *all* forms. Today, to retain full membership in the Crisis of the Month Club, there is every prospect that our theologians shall begin to inquire into the "anatomy of violence" and to write papers and conduct seminars on "theology and violence," or even the "theology *of* violence." We may expect to be instructed in the linguistic distinctions in the Old and New Testaments between "to kill" and "to murder," just as we have been told about alleged distinctions between "just" and "unjust" wars.

But like most detours of the great god Relevance, it is in reality a dead-end. The question of violence is not clarified by "anatomies" of violence, theologies of violence, or etymologies of "to murder" and "to kill." Moreover, all this pandering to the god of Relevance can neither mitigate nor direct racial violence, any more than it can tell us anything really "new" about violence. Racial violence is at this moment beyond the powers of anyone or anything—the President, Rap Brown, the National Guard, RAM, and tear gas—to control or direct. The fact is that it is now pointless to ask how we can avoid violence. The only questions now are: How *much* violence will there be, and what *form* and *direction* will it take? Nonetheless, the rat control bill, attacks on the poverty program, the decision to build an ABM system, the passion for riot control bills in the Congress and the states, the determination to spend $3 billion a month in Vietnam if necessary, the training of the National Guard for duty as domestic police, and compacts between the states to trade off these troops—all this portends that the principal course government and politics will continue to pursue to "solve" racism is a violent one—that is, the employment of all the men necessary and all the techniques of modern warfare available to suppress and contain the resistance of black people to the American ghetto of squalor, despair, inhumanity and hopelessness.

Any Christian witness against violence must begin, therefore, where it left off eighteen, and maybe twenty, centuries ago: a witness against *any* use of violence to solve political and social problems that would destroy the lives of political and social opponents. Politics is means, not Messiah, because life is more—indeed, other—than politics. Should the intellectuals (accepting the faggots thrown in by the theologians) offer an ideology of violence to the black community of America, and should the black community accept it, the "final solution" of the "black problem" would be provided by the honkies. To think that violence can redirect the white community's racism into the brotherhood of man is to capitulate before the ideology of the honkies, and in the end to become a honky. To think that violence can redirect enmity into brotherhood is to ignore the most obvious "lesson" of Vietnam. But to say this, to plead that violence cannot alter America's racism, is not a message of "non-violence" from the Christian community (largely white and middle class) to the black community (largely impoverished and oppressed); it is rather a message to the government and politics of our nation (largely white and middle class) to desist from launching an attempt to solve this nation's racial crises by violence.

An even greater danger in the obsession with violence is the faith that racial violence will somehow become organized, widespread, effectively destroy meaningful property (and probably lives) and paralyze a large segment of American society, so that "something" will *have* to be done. But the evidence so far is heavily against it, especially against the faith that the "something" will be conciliatory. The evidence so far is that *if* a segment of America were somehow paralyzed by a violent uprising, the "something" that followed would be so oppressive and complete as to commit this nation irrevocably to a proud, and legalized, apartheid police state.

Is this sort of overt violence the final direction our racism is apt to take? Does not the evidence so far suggest the contrary? Instead of the great conflagration inciting "something" to be done, is not another pattern already discernible? Watts, and pacification by police, Marines and the National Guard. Pause. Next, Newark and Detroit, and pacification by police and National Guard. Pause. After perhaps six months, or nine months, Cleveland and San Francisco, and more pacification. Pause. Next, Milwaukee and Jacksonville, or perhaps Columbia, S.C., or maybe Waycross, Ga., and more pacification. Pause. And so on, with each uprising like the preceding one, capricious, irrational, small-scale, without plans or strategies relating one action to another, and unorganized in its initiation and early phase. A city or two one week—repression, pause, nothing noticeably altered anywhere except in the devastation of the pacified area which is, relatively speaking, small and insignificant. Then three months later, two towns and a large city—repression, pause, nothing noticeably altered anywhere. Perhaps a leader is killed and another disappears, but nothing noticeable. There's plenty of color TV, plenty of bombs on Vietnam, plenty of strikes, plenty of debates over taxes, but nothing is noticeably altered anywhere.

But each repression becomes more efficient because the technicians in the police control points have all the apparatus to heighten and perfect the repression—in a word, to make the repression technically more efficient and the pause less noticeable, more normal. Justice? It's identical with the law that upholds *our* (white) order and protects *our* property and ensures the safety of *our* streets. (After all, *that* was the real issue in 1968.) Plans have already been discussed at governors' conferences about exchanging units of the National Guard: Memphis is closer to Little Rock than to Nashville; Philadelphia is closer to New York than to Pittsburgh. Regionalism will work under the right kinds of pressure. Moreover, a malicious Chief Executive could always have the telegraph lines tied up in order to spotlight a governor's inability to deal forcefully with a crisis. From the Pentagon to the sheriff's office in Neshoba County, the technicians have all the apparatus to rationalize racial uprisings by black citizens. It has to do with the technical mentality of the American people, with the technical efficiency of the police, with cybernation, with self-correcting mechanisms, as each uprising feeds information about itself into the machine. The machine learns, remembers (in a way that humans will not), and knows what and how to do better "next time," and the public is satisfied because it is not personally or materially inconvenienced. To expect the great conflagration to get us out of our racism, or in the 20th century to expect a genuine crisis to catapult us violently into the police state is to indulge in fantasy. Rather, we will be—or, more accurately, are being—computerized into the technological police state *at our own doing*; it is the only way law and order today can protect the property and maintain the order of the white establishment.

Hence—in contrast to the great conflagration producing a dramatic "something" that redeems or damns—we shall be denied the advantage of being surprised one gray morning to wake up and find ourselves in the concentration camp of the technological era. The chief characteristic of the technological police state is that it is our own doing, our own work, our own achievement, our "Final Solution"—that, and the absence of any overt, dramatic event or sign that we, blithely oblivious to the fact, are being eased into the technological concentration camp. Not Auschwitz, not Dachau, but the Secular City: convenience, order and respectability.

In everything that has happened between Watts and Detroit, this pattern is more obvious than the pattern suggesting the great conflagration into "something." We ignore it at our peril. Police methods and the use of violence by government and politics have become so rationalized and effective in advanced industrial-technological societies that it is difficult to envision a genuine crisis—that is, an overt and violent event that forces a change in either direction—by conflagration. After all, the charge that the "authorities" leveled most often against the police and National Guard operations in Newark and Detroit was inefficiency, not injustice and brutality. The brave new world, the Secular City of 1984, will not result from a gigantic and damning crisis provoking us to this eventuality, for such a crisis might conceivably force a reversal of the direction of our racism. The real "crisis" of the technological era is *that there is no crisis,* no conflagration and violence to provoke "something."

Perhaps William Faulkner's saga of Flem and the other Snopes is the most accurate vision yet of the technological era —a vision that begins, lest we forget, with the "barn burning" (and the threats to burn barns) of Flem's daddy. (And perhaps this vision of Snopes stands in sharpest contradiction to Faulkner's own profession of faith that "man will prevail"—if that man is Flem Snopes who is marked by what he wrought in his communities during his lifetime.)

For in the technological society Snopes is in charge. And the Snopes of Snopes is to seek respectability—not justice, not virtue, but respectability—and thereby to gain power and control and money. But the Snopes of Snopes is to seek respectability by *not* provoking a crisis by conflagration, by *not* burning a barn, by *not* committing murder—or by *not* being caught. To do otherwise—to fall into the failure of a crisis by conflagration, to get caught at barn burning—is to threaten the very respectability which the Snopes of the industrial-technological society must have to maintain himself and his order. Snopes and technique fail when they ignite or cannot rationalize a conflagration, a genuine crisis. But while Flem is murdered, what he is and what he did cannot be killed.

It was not the immorality but rather the inefficiency of Johnson's war policy in Vietnam that made possible the mass-ing of significant dissent from mainstream America—including, especially, the dissent heard from the universities and the Church. The explanation for this is simple: mainstream America had neither the tradition nor the perspective from which to criticize the "immorality" of the Vietnam war or *any* war. University and Church were hostages to the political messianism of the 20th century. What dissent there was (and is) could be mounted only when the quick resolution of the war did not follow from the fantastic tandem of escalation bombing and search-and-destroy missions—a policy which Johnson switched on, but which he did not conceive. In any event, following what they learned from the pattern of how to handle the "all deliberate speed" of fifteen years ago, the bureaucracy simply wore the agitation out. The bureaucracy had nowhere to go; the agitation did: ecology, woman's liberation, etc., etc.

And what, after all, is the real horror of My Lai (called "Pinkville" by the Army)? Not the women and babies ripped apart by the most advanced weaponry of technology's arsenal in the hands of American boys carrying out America's policies. Not that. We have had plenty of that put before us by the scholars and newsmen and photographers reporting about our victims in North and South Vietnam, Korea, the Dominican Republic, Tokyo, Hiroshima and Nagasaki; any part of it would equal what was found in My Lai, with no official expressions of horror and no threats of courts-martial or even of a war crime tribunal. Not that. My Lai is the image of women and babies ripped apart at point-blank range, their eyes terrorized and incredible, staring into the eyes of their American executioners inches away. *That* is the horror of My Lai. Not the *victims* of our decisions. The victims of Hiroshima and Nagasaki and Hanoi and Saigon are just as grotesque, but senators and congressmen and citizens had no public complaints about those victims disturbing their stomach juices. The image of *how* it happened at My Lai—point-blank, American boys, terrorized eyes, mutilated babies—that is the image we cannot live with in the technological era. It is not the same image as bombers launched from the technological marvel of aircraft carriers, dispatched by radar, blessed by Christ's own. That is the image we can live with—the morally isolated image, two miles up from the ripped and bleeding victims, American boys staring not into their bedumbed and pleading eyes inches away, but peering through oxygen-filled masks into the gadgets, dials, needles, buttons, switches and radar. That is clean, like our image of pastel-tiled bathrooms. We can live with that image. And that is what it means to live in the technological era. Snopes, like the Bible, teaches that the punishment fits the crime.

The Christian must learn to live in a technological concentration camp controlled by Snopes and his ideology of respectability, an integral part of said respectability being a member of the Church as well as president of the bank. Any way "out" must begin, therefore, with an understanding of the nature of the victory of Snopes and technique. The victory of Snopes, as the victory of technique, is the achievement of results by indirection, by the use of science, by maneuver (which might also include "rumors" of barn burning), by calculation and reason guided by the values of efficiency and effectiveness and permeated with respectability, by seeing that the barricades are never stormed, by permitting only pseudo-crises, not real crises, and by having the community accept Snopes as "Mister" without thinking to ask itself: "When did we begin to call him Mister?"

"Where is the Good News in all this?" Where it has always been. God's death by violence on the cross and his victory in the resurrection were not the result of the triumph of our violence, of our provocation of a crisis or manipulation of a pseudo-crisis, but the victory of *his* Word. And this is just about all that can be said. Yes, there are signs to be discerned. The punishment fits the crime. The inevitable resort to violence to crush ghetto uprisings against the sins of centuries thrusts us, black and white, straightaway into the technological concentration camp of contemporary society. The violence that has been part of the tradition and cult of our history, and which our academicians and theologians may yet raise into the cult of technological

Violence and Snopes

violence as have their brothers and cousins in government and politics, now renders any modification of white racism almost impossible. And the technology we created and worship, as the children of Israel created and worshiped the golden calf, will provide the "Final Solution" for both blacks and whites in America as we are computed at our own insistence into the society of Snopes.

But the Good News is still "here." Perhaps the only way we will ever discern the reality, the very existence of the concentration camp in our technological, color-TV, interstate-highway, pastel-bathroom, jet-age, "nice" civilization, is from the cross. Perhaps the only way now that we will ever know the Snopes of Snopes of us all—that the Snopes of Snopes is not "white trash" but what has happened to all of us in our passion to redeem ourselves—perhaps the only way now we will ever know that we too are judged and reconciled by God, is to recognize Snopes and ourselves in the light of the victory of the resurrected Christ.

X
A Homily on Patriotism

We do not need to wait for the prophets or social analysts to tell us that we are living through the end of one era and the beginning of another. That is the most obvious fact of our times. The foundations of everything in the old order have been shattered; they can no longer sustain the old structures—and this means the structures of both religious and political institutions, the institutions of Church and State.

Obviously, the point of departure for any account of "patriotism" is the Christian's obedience to God. Allegiance to God must determine the kind of obedience to the State. But when both the Church and the political structures are being changed before our eyes, the problem of patriotism assumes a new dimension, and we must be careful not to fall for the huckster's pitch that newness is the same as goodness and that whatever is contemporary is right. There is no support for this point of view in the Bible, or in history. The Bible warns about idolizing any period of time, "modern times" included. Any effort to be serious about the question of patriotism in 1970 must begin with the fact of the end of the old order and the emergence of a new one, of the end of the old institutions of State and Church and the formation of new ones. Consequently, we must first determine whether we can discern, however dimly, the character of the new institutions of both Church and State which are emerging out of the disintegration of the old ones. We need to do this to avoid the danger of engaging in platitudes about patriotism which, in effect, compromise the obedience due to both God and the State. Then we can consider how we are to obey God rather than men in the face of the new realities of State and Church which confront the Christian at the end of the 20th century.

We believe that it is possible to discern the direction which the institutions of State and Church are taking, as well as their principal characteristics in the next generation or so. The picture is not a reassuring one to those of us schooled in the traditions of liberal democracy, and in a more or less liberal approach to the relation of the Church to democracy, identified as God's "way for all mankind in political matters." But we must at the same time recall the bankruptcy of so-called "conservative" thought to meet the crisis brought about by the end of liberal democracy.

The feature of the State which today is a blatant contradiction of our textbook definitions of the democratic process is, in our view, the feature that will be most characteristic of the State of the next generations: the bureaucratic, impersonal, technological entity which remains impervious to elections or changes of political party or administration or personnel—in a word, immune to the democratic process itself. Concomitant with this are the ever-increasing tasks assumed by or imposed upon the bureaucracy, which is now, in reality and in fact, the State. The State is not the enlightened electorate (if it ever was), nor is it the politicians, who come and go without making any significant difference in the ways of the bureaucratic State. (One need only consider the insignificant differences among the Truman, Eisenhower, Kennedy, Johnson and Nixon administrations, or the eternal presence of J. Edgar Hoover and the satraps in the State Department and Foreign Service, to understand the most obvious manifestations of the modern State.) Moreover, what is fundamental in the so-called Communist states is likewise fundamental in the so-called "free world" states: the citizens of both demand that the State (i.e., the bureaucracy which remains as the politicians come

A Homily on Patriotism 105

and go) assume the responsibility for solving and directing all the activities of mankind. With the enthusiastic support of all citizens and all communities and enterprises (especially the communications media) within the State, politics claims to be the most important reality today. Consequently, the demands of the State are well-nigh total. Recall the election slogans of 1968—slogans which demonstrated more than anything else the identity of interest of the major political parties. Said one: "*This time, vote as if your whole world depended on it.*" Said the other: "*There is no alternative.*" These are not the slogans of Orwell's 1984; they were in fact the sole platforms of both of the major political parties. Moreover, these slogans express very clearly the unwitting character of the creeping totalitarianism of the modern State, in both the "communist" and the "free world," a totalitarianism supported by the peculiarity of mass participation of the citizenry in politics, from income taxes to Social Security payments to no-option requirement of television attendance at political conventions and elections and Apollo moon shots. It is the unwitting, but nonetheless mass-based, character of 20th-century totalitarianism that makes it the more serious, the more dangerous, the more difficult to oppose. If there were a plot of Machiavellian-type conspirators (communist or fascist or racist), the problem would not be as serious as it is, nor the solution so remote. The heart of our political crisis today is the determination of citizens to turn to the State for all answers, and the willingness of the technique-directed, bureaucratic State to direct all aspects of the life of man. This is the environment in which the Christian must obey God and not man, the environment in which the Christian grapples with the issues of patriotism.

Is it possible to discern the direction which the Church is taking in this environment? We think so, and we believe that the direction is one which compounds the crisis about patriotism for the Christian. For most of those institutions of the Church which are charged with relating the Christian to the social and political implications of Christianity have accepted as normal this new role of the State in the affairs of mankind. Protestantism especially in recent years has unwittingly supported the growing power of the State by uncritically following the lead of the State in its definitions of social and political ills and in its solutions for those ills. (This is the real meaning of the death-of-God movement.) In a word, Protestantism has abdicated to the State the responsibility for directing the actions of Christians in the political and social order. The two most obvious examples of this that may be cited are war and racism.

With few exceptions the Church supported both world wars for the very same reasons laid down by the various States involved on both sides of the conflict. The Church gave no warnings in life and word about the Gospel's renunciation of force as the solution to human problems, thus rejecting the reality of the cross and the resurrection, God's triumph of life over death. We in the Church should have given witness in the life of our congregations (or, as the World Council of Churches would intone, in our "Faith and Order") to the victory of life over death, of reconciliation over annihilation. Instead, we permitted the State alone to place the issues of war and peace before us and before mankind, and we in the Church made our decisions on war and peace on the terms laid down by the State. This is a clear abdication of the calling of Christians. But this is why the Church's witness against war—especially the Vietnam war—is equivocal and therefore taken seriously by very few, whether inside or outside the Church.

Moreover, having supported for centuries in the life of our congregations a segregationist view of the kingdom of God, our witness was in clear and open violation of Christ's victory over sin and death. For that reason, American churches have in the past decade been able to do little more than exhaust their witness to the oneness of all men in Christ by a half-hearted (and largely professionalist) support of Supreme Court decisions and the legalistic redundancies of civil rights laws. The churches gave a militant opposition to match the overt and blatant racism of the South, ignoring or blinded to the racism in the churches and Lions Clubs and ghettos and schools in the North, where it was a more entrenched, insidious and effective denial of the oneness of all men in Christ. As a result the Church has been unable to offer any alternative *in its own life* to the de facto racism throughout the United States.

The Church's testimony, rather than turning us from the idolatry of political power and a blasphemous patriotism which calls upon the State to do and to direct everything, has unwittingly supported the trend toward the absolutism of State power, in effect counseling Christians to render to Caesar the things that are God's—and thereby making it impossible to render to the State the service that is due the State. It is significant—nay, critical—for Christians to realize that this action of the Church is just the reverse of what the Church of the 4th and 5th centuries did in the face of another, less subtle and dangerous, move toward State absolutism. Charles Norris Cochrane's classic, *Christianity and Classical Culture,* records the Church's opposition to the "creative politics" of the Augustan empire, a politics which insisted "that it was possible to attain a goal of permanent security, peace and freedom through political action. . . . This notion the Christians denounced with uniform vigor and consistency. To them the State, far from being the supreme instrument of human emancipation and perfectibility, was a straightjacket to be justified at best as a 'remedy for sin.' To think of it otherwise they considered the grossest of superstitions." Today, we find ourselves face to face with the crisis, compounded by the Church's own counsels of support, that the early Christians considered "the grossest of superstitions." That is why the Church, especially in its social action, is today the leading practitioner of the death-of-God theology.

The political consequences—one might say "the patriotic consequences"—of this current mood of the Church's relationship to the State are a great illusion. The Church is supporting a relationship to the State which has no basis in the truth of the Gospel. As the French Christian, Jacques Ellul, writes: "To think of everything as political, to conceal everything by using this word . . . to place everything in the hands of the State, to appeal to the State in all circumstances, to subordinate the problems of the individual to those of the group, to believe that political affairs are on everybody's level and that everybody is qualified to deal with them—these factors characterize the politicization of modern man and, as such, comprise a myth." Might it not be that the Church's faith in this myth, rather than in its crucified and resurrected Lord, will be the factor that tips the scales and inches the Western world into the modern totalitarian State, the technological concentration camps, into (again Ellul) "an organization of objects, run by objects"?

Here is the critical point of the Christian witness today about "patriotism." Here is where our old clichés about "my country right or wrong" and "for God and country" and "things of the spirit for God, things of the earth for the State," are rendered not only irrelevant, but insidious. We must be guided by the New Testament and not by the State (or the Church) on the issue of patriotism. Only then will we be able to grasp the nature of the temptation to possess "all the kingdoms of the world in their glory" set before Jesus by the devil himself. "All these," the devil said, "I will give you, if you will only fall down and do me homage" (Lk. 4, 6-7). First, we must note that Jesus does not deny the devil's claim that he is able to deliver "all the kingdoms of the world in their glory" to anyone who will "do homage" to Satan! While this promise of the devil does not mean that "the kingdoms of the world in their glory" are necessarily in his power, it does mean that "worldly kingdoms," because of the seemingly absolute power they wield over men and nations, are tempted "in their glory" to do homage to Satan and put themselves at his beck and call. This is a judgment that undercuts a great deal of the rhetoric about the liberal democratic State, as well as today's so-called Christian realism. "Worldly kingdoms" can deny God and serve themselves and the devil instead of mankind, but they cannot "kill" God or remove themselves from his sovereignty, judgment and love.

When we grasp this, Jesus' answer becomes a pattern for patriotism which neither abjures politics nor does homage to Satan through political activity: "Begone, Satan! Scripture says, 'You shall do homage to the Lord your God and worship him alone'" (Mt. 4, 8-10).

Even more to the point, perhaps, is that as we live and work we must remember that Peter, "replying for himself and the apostles," *spoke to officials of religious institutions, not political institutions* when he said: "We must obey God rather than men" (Acts 5, 30). Religious institutions have no monopoly on the gift of the Holy Spirit; indeed, as Scripture makes clear, often it is just the contrary. The witness of religious institutions on this question of "patriotism" is misleading and dangerous to both Christians and the State whenever Christians are encouraged to believe that their only witness in the political order is to involve themselves in the very political processes which, wittingly and without any conspiracy, are easing us toward a 20th-century totalitarianism more complete and more effective than anything yet experienced by man. Again we cite Ellul: "All civilizations have imposed a certain amount of restriction, but they left man in a large field for free and individual action. The Roman slave, the medieval serf, was freer, more personal, more socially human (I do not say 'happier,' from the material point of view) *than the modern industrial worker or the Soviet Union official*" (italics ours).

It is within the power of the modern State—East and West, communist and "free world"—to be what no other State in history could be: totalitarian, exerting effective and almost total control over the life of man. That is why the Church and Christians risk idolatry when they urge the medium of any of the contemporary political processes as the best or only vehicle for expressing Christ's victory over every power that separates men, whether that power be social injustice, racism, politics, war or poverty. To urge contemporary political activity as the best way to witness to Christ in the social order is to accept politics and not Christ as Messiah. It is scarcely an alternative to a narrow and bigoted patriotism. Indeed, it is no "patriotism" at all, because there is no service to the State if the Christian is merely to sanction the very processes and decisions which the State has already taken, and which are moving us gradually but inexorably toward modern totalitarianism.

It remains only to say that the call of Christ is not a call for a repudiation of political affairs. Such a repudiation cannot be carried through, any more than we can stop breathing or reject the gift of speech. Moreover, there are Christ's own words about God and Caesar; there is his crucifixion under Pontius Pilate; there are Paul's injunctions about being subject to the governing authorities and praying for the State! The question is how seriously we take the political effort, and how we view the contemporary political process. The question is whether the State, in the figure of Pilate, had the last word over Jesus Christ. If so, we should continue our present course of exhausting our witness to the State by supporting all State programs, in the death-of-God faith that only politics can resolve human ills. If not, we must devise ways to insist upon the relative character of political life, and thereby witness to the idolatrous character of a political style which claims to do and to direct everything for man. Christians in their communities must somehow become independent of the State in order to render the only service to the State that Christians as Christians can render: preaching the Word that God, not politics, is redeemer. This will require, as a minimum, a fresh look at what *is* political action today, remaining wide open to the probability that most of what the State defines as political today is an illusion, a subterfuge. Christians ought to become communities which witness by their life to the truth that "God has made of one blood all nations of men"—surely a more effective witness against racism than a confused and halting support of civil rights legislation. Christians ought to have witness and worship which sends forth the Good News that the sixth commandment is not an ideal but a fact, and that life, not death, reconciliation, not war, is the truth about man, because it is the truth given to man by Jesus Christ.

XI
Up to Our Steeples in Politics

We believe that everyone—political figure or commentator, citizen or alien, man or woman, black or white, conservative or radical—who at this particular time says that this people and this nation are in deep, perhaps irremediable political trouble, speaks the truth.

We also wish to speak of politics. But we will be repeating, restating, rehashing (but not revising) what we have been trying to say about these crises for several years. Stated simply, we believe that the fundamental crises in our land arise from the obsession with politics, the faith that the political order is the *only* source and authority from which we can and ought to seek relief from what ails us as a community and as individuals. Because there is in our land no real challenge to these obsessions, we believe that our crises will deepen, perhaps even beyond a point of no return, and that we shall become citizens of a technological police state because of the prevalent concept that a full use of political force and cunning is the only resource we have to guarantee freedom and human dignity. Cases in point are the more than 70 percent of our good people who approved the police work in Chicago during the week of the 1968 Democratic convention—undoubtedly the same people who were horrified at Sheriff Clark's work in Selma in 1965—and the effectiveness of "violence, crime in the streets, protestors and dissent" in the 1968 election campaign. This suggests that while the technological barriers for the enclosure may not yet have been perfected, we are probably already inside the compound, and that our identification cards are already being notched, with food allotments and medical services in some stage of preparation.

Look at us! Politics prevails, and everyone believes that this is the only way it can be. Political troubles, political programs, political crises and political figures are all that count, and all that should count. The White House launches Vice President Spiro Agnew on a desperate crusade because "news" is what matters. Art, drama, novels, essays, poems, religion, dance, architecture, beads, pendants, psychedelia—to be real, every energy must somehow relate to politics. If not, it is irrelevant, not serious, obscurantist, old-fashioned, fundamentalist, sectarian, cloistered, a form of lunacy. Caesar is messiah; we are bones, sinew and *politics,* period. Politics tells us what we shall do with our bones and our sinew. There is nothing wrong with us or our communities that political revolution, reordering, restructuring and reestablishing cannot overcome. How could we believe otherwise?

But perhaps what we are talking about is not new in the Western political tradition. Perhaps all this is simply a more extreme manifestation of robust and healthy Western politics. We believe not. We are convinced of the basic accuracy of the social analyses of Jacques Ellul, the French Christian, who makes an overpowering case that because our environment is now technique, not nature, the political implications are that technique and bureaucracy, not an exchange of ideas in political debates and elections, are the stuff of politics today. And this is unprecedented. As Ellul explains, "The decisions fundamentally affecting the future of a nation are in the domains of technology, fiscal technique, or police methods . . . fruits of the technician's labors." Politics in the traditional sense is an "illusion."

We have talked about these phenomena in this volume as political messianism, politics-as-Baal and technological concentration camps. Politics, a means to *an* end—justice—has become *the* end. We have been duped into believing that whatever ails us is tractable and can be cured only by political and social nostrums. God knows that there is much wrong with us politically, and the proper goal of political action is the adjustment of external and relative arrangements, laws and institutions so that they function as instruments of social justice for all. But just here is the political tragedy, for what *is* wrong with us politically cannot be corrected as long as we insist by our political action that politics can correct *everything* that is wrong with us. To argue, as almost everyone does, "If politics cannot cure our every social ill, nothing can," is not to offer an alternative to what we are saying, but to define the nature of our tragedy. We are convinced that this argument is one very important reason why the very proper political (although constitutionally redundant) efforts in the so-called civil rights era failed to adjust political, social and economic structures to meet the racial and social discrimination that had been welling up because of our racist tradition and advanced technological civilization. The ideology of the left and right, conservative and liberal, drew strength from the same myth: that the constraint of the police, law, federal marshals, national guards and bureaucracy (national, state and local) together with the largesse of the federal budget was *all* that was necessary—indeed, *all* that could be done—to end a crisis that political adjustment could improve but not overcome. Racism is something which political adjustment could ease and ameliorate, but only if Caesar admitted his inherent limitation— not as an excuse for inaction, but as a reason for action. However, pushed beyond its obvious point of effectiveness, politics in what Ellul calls the "technological society" could, by its unfilled promises, only exacerbate minority alienation and majority impatience and frustration, and in the end be used in a clearly totalitarian fashion by Caesar to impose its prejudice on the recalcitrants. Politics alone could not end the crisis, and did not.

Examples? Specifics? What about those voices a scant four years ago shrieking for massive intervention by troops, marshals, money and all the rest of the political power of Caesar, especially his federal apparatus, to cure the *South's* racism—the same voices now shrieking for moderation and restraint in Caesar's use of his police power? Or what about the contrast between 1954 and 1970? In 1954, the voices called for law and order and for obedience to the "law of the land, however distasteful"; in 1970, the same voices say that a call for law and order is a call for racism.

Perhaps, as some believe, the civil rights activity of the 1960's was no more than an effort to ease the consciences of liberals who had no intention of altering their patronizing attitude toward black men if it would cost them a lot of money or jeopardize their (or their children's) status in the country club or with the Establishment. But the real point is that the liberal conscience *was* susceptible of being soothed by laws and executive orders because it had been cast in a tradition convinced that contradictions to the "beloved community" could be overcome by political activity, guided by the enlightened opinion of a populace and educated into the values of the prevailing political consensus.

As long as this nation persists in the belief that there are no limits to what politics can do for us, it is inevitable that we shall try to tear each other asunder, breaking off into disillusioned and hateful factions, all of us with our own political nostrum which we shall brutally inflict upon those who do not share our nostrum because they have ones of their own. And all this will occur in a political environment which Kierkegaard would call "sick unto death," because no one will laugh at the regular and religious incantations about "in God we trust" or at the pious rhetoric about the greatest and most powerful nation in the history of the world being forged by a free press, free speech, constitutional government and the two-party system.

What we are confronting today is political messianism, Baalism. In this regard, let us be specific. For a number of years now we have tried to say to the Christian and to the Church that an exclusive reliance on the political processes of the 20th century will exacerbate these very processes to the point that we will compute ourselves into the technological concentration camp. "But they came to Baal-peor, and consecrated themselves to Baal and became detestable like the thing they loved" (Hos. 9, 10). We have tried to explain not only why this is a political calamity of an unparalleled order, but why it is blasphemous for Christians to exhaust their witness to the world in the processes Caesar determines for us. "The sure consequence," we have said, "of relying exclusively on law and politics to resolve America's racism will be the confirmation of that racism *in* and *by* our legal and political system."

The political activity of the ecumenical movement, social agencies and seminaries of mainline (and most sectarian) Protestantism, regardless of their theological orientation, has in large part been expressions of just this Baalism. We have accepted with little or no objection the judgment about the crises and the lists of priorities offered up by Caesar, the political order. Cold wars and wars of insurrection, racism, poverty, urban decay, etc.—such is the terminology of Caesar. But God's vicars in denominational social agencies, seminaries, pulpits and religious journals have merely lined themselves and their constituency, money and manpower behind Caesar's definition of the issues facing the nation and the people. As if they, God's ambassadors, had nothing to say *as* God's ambassadors about man's nature and destiny, and how that might well assign a different set of priorities. As if obedience to God demanded a realism that waited with shaking hands and bated breath for the latest white paper on the latest crisis from the State Department, the latest views of the current justices of the Supreme Court, the latest study from the Labor or Agriculture Departments, and the latest bulletin or in-depth report from the worldwide facilities of NBC News. As if the inhabitants of the white ghettos, north and south, rural and mountain and urban, were inhuman, without souls, subjects neither of God's grace and the Church's compassion nor of the liberal's largesse, and not children of God who had also been impoverished and dehumanized by the affluence and the gimmickry of the liberal, political-military, economic Establishment. As if the real and *only* enemies of Christ were the jeering and spitting and sometimes murdering rednecks and mountaineers, transplanted to Dayton or New Orleans or Cleveland, who give forth no newborn, bury no dead, share none of the hopes and dreads, joys and anguishes of the affluent, educated and cultured product of the liberal system of politics, economics and education. As if no enemy can be found in the wicked economic and social system—as it looks from the bottom: in the paper mills and cotton mills and marginal filling stations, in the honky-tonks, crossroad stores, sheriff offices and police headquarters, in the poolrooms, labor unions, service clubs, church missionary circles and political systems. As if the Christian Church were a folk church *only* in the South. As if no enemy exists in the vapid, starved, politically subservient, century-old, ineffective educational system which maliciously imposes a new brand of 20th-century totalitarianism on the politically and economically helpless, the serfs of the affluent American. As if Christ's vicars had received a commandment to show only contempt and loathing, never compassion, for those whose economic and political powerlessness in their own ghettos and hollows and red-clay farms and subdivisions made them immune and hostile and at times violent when faced with the threats of the federal enemy and the blandishments and intimidations and hatreds of liberal Christian activists.

God's prophets, not unlike Zedekiah, the son of Chenaanah (1 Kgs. 22), are being cued and set in motion by Caesar, and away go their love gifts of money, personnel, new seminary curriculum and what little moral suasion the social agency could muster in the tract-racks at St. John's-by-the-Gas-Station and Boiling-Springs-Emmanuel-Church-at-the-Crossroads! Was it segregation in the schools? Or the freedom rides? Or the sit-ins? Or voter rights? Or peace in Vietnam (never Cuba or Latin America or the Middle East)? The witness of Christ's reconciliation was exhausted by supporting the (more or less) liberal political orientation of Caesar. The Good News became the legislative, court and administrative victories of the liberal movements, usually at the expense of those who could ill afford another political or economic defeat—the ghetto black or ghetto white. The Good News was McCarthy's victory in New Hampshire, or Senator Kennedy's decision "to enter," or President Johnson's decision to "stay out," or some hanky-panky with some draft cards, or peace talks in Paris and Helsinki, etc., etc., etc.

We have learned *nothing*. A few years ago we were told that a vote for Goldwater was a vote for some sort of manifestation of anti-Christ (the sort depended on where you lived), and so Christians, from bishops to the omnipresent concerned laymen, spent themselves electing, in the name of Christ crucified and resurrected, Lyndon Baines Johnson, heir apparent to John Fitzgerald Kennedy.

The political consequences of the death-of-God movement have always been its most significant and long-range manifestation. But the manifestation is completely misunderstood unless we realize that the theological expression of the death of God simply ratifies what has been in fact the sole witness to society and politics of the Church of Jesus Christ in the United States for decades. We quote from a death-of-God manifesto: "It is not an optimism of grace, but a worldly optimism. . . . It faces despair not with the conviction that out of it God can bring hope, but with the conviction that the human conditions that created it can be overcome, whether those conditions be poverty, discrimination, or mental illness." This credo of the most publicized of the death-of-God theologians actually describes the totality of the recent witness of the Body of Jesus Christ against man's murder, here and abroad, of the one who was made his brother by the resurrection of the same Jesus Christ. Surely there is another way—that is, if God is not dead. Surely our calling as Christians is not summed up by a vapid, pathetic and generally ineffective effort to inject morality and high-mindedness into political activity.

Our apostasy, therefore, is fundamentally the same one that St. Paul struck down in Antioch (cf. Galatians 1–2), for our *actions* stamp our doctrines as heretical. Thomas Merton wrote that "to reconcile man with man and not with God is to reconcile no one at all." How, in the face of the last 2,000 years or 200 years or two months or two weeks, can we dispute the validity of that judgment? We are idolators, we are Baal worshipers, because we have rendered to Caesar the things that are God's and thereby have been unable to render to Caesar the things that are his. We have identified the witness to Christ's reconciliation with the effort of law and order (Caesar) as the sole means to effect better human relations. For what other reason has ecumenical, mainline white Protestantism despised a witness to the impoverished white ghetto (despite black people's support of the effort) and become increasingly wary and disenchanted about maintaining (or beginning new) witnesses to impoverished black and Puerto Rican and Mexican American ghettos? The social action of mainline Protestantism, more so than the rhetoric of the death-of-God movement, has confessed by its deeds that God is dead; Christian social action, more so than the rhetoric of the death-of-God movement, has faced "despair not with the conviction that out of it God can bring hope, but with the conviction that the human conditions that created it can be overcome, whether those conditions be poverty, discrimination, or mental illness." And that is why we Christians are in apostasy, and why we cannot as Christians render to Caesar the things that are Caesar's. We are sanctioning the efforts of Caesar to do the one thing that Caesar cannot do: to be God and redeem man from sin and death.

All this is why we do not believe that we are reactionary or fashionable when we observe in print that it bothers us to see preachers, nuns, priests and other clergy up to their gills in politics, and especially in political conventions. Ours is simply a question derived from the fundamental question we are here raising: Is obedience to Christ exhausted by immersing oneself in Caesar's definition of politics? Is witness to Christ's victory uniting all men best made by service to what *Caesar* judges as the urgent issues of our times? Might it not be that Caesar himself is confused, or is lying? There is evidence in the history of Western civilization to support both affirmations.

Might it not be that, wittingly or unwittingly, Caesar is diverting the Christian (and everyone else, for that matter) from an onslaught on the real centers of action by insisting that *he,* and he alone, is the one to define the critical issues of human life?

Before all this be read off as typical American fundamentalism or modern Mennonitism or whatever, we hasten to explain that we, too, came through the liberal-to-neo-orthodox theological era, and we did it in what was then and is now considered to be the finest Ivy League tradition. That is not to boast (and maybe it is to apologize). It is to say that we have been exposed to and indoctrinated by the view that the principal Christian vocation in the 20th century is to go where the action is—that is, into the muck and mire of politics, controversy and "human existence wherever it is."

We were told that in order to be honest to our vocation, in order to be a Christian minister in the world-come-of-age, we had to become as knowledgeable in banking as John K. Galbraith and Merrill Lynch, as wise in international affairs as George Kennan, Henry Kissinger, Hans Morgenthau, Dean Acheson, Dean Rusk and John Foster Dulles, as expert in political science as David B. Truman and Robert E. Lane, as bright in sociology as Talcott Parsons and Robert Merton, and as learned in psychology as Erik Erikson and Anna Freud. Unless, of course, we were to minister to a rural church, in which case we should know the 4-H Club pledge, be acquainted with the best theories of rural economics, and undertake agricultural and community surveys superior to the ones done by the county agent.

The evangelical notion of "winning them one by one" was the source of many humorous remarks in the lecture halls, recreation rooms and refectories. And we agreed, for we knew, from rides home after Sunday school listening to our parents quarreling about the grocery money, that culture would win them back faster than we as the Lord's spokesmen could win them or keep them. We missed the key, however: that what the evangelical notion was all about was what we were winning them *to,* and what culture was winning them *from.* A change of method or tactics in winning them may have been less important than a change in the concept of what winning them really meant. The theologians told us about the cultural imperialism that was inextricably a part of the 19th-century individualism of "winning them one by one," but this turned out later on to have been less real for us than the cultural imperialism of the Gospel of "relevance-and-realism," being won over by the decision-makers, a culture, a political party, an entire industry, etc.

Be that as it may, we returned to the South armed with Gunnar Myrdal and V. O. Key in one hand and Calhoun's *Lecture Notes* in the other. The Bible and Calvin's *Institutes* remained in the packing boxes until the awed laymen could get over to build the bookshelves in our "study." We were ready to go into the muck and the mire of politics and social controversy, to meet human existence wherever it was. We were set with many plans of how to do battle with the devil, although nine-tenths of us were convinced that there wasn't such a thing, for what we remembered best about "Introduction to the English New Testament" was what demythologizing had disclosed about the social irrelevance of the three-storied world-view of biblical times.

Now, today, our questions have to do with the location of politics, or, at any rate, where we are supposed to go. As they say, where is the action? Where is the real politics, the muck and the mire, the site of human existence? Is it found where they told us to look for it—election politics (in one of the two or three or four parties)? In surveys to rival those of the county agent and the welfare workers? In Talcott Parsons? In supporting the forces of law and order because the Supreme Court initiated Christ's interest in man's inhumanity to man?

Fifteen years ago the American Church was enjoined by its leaders, experts and theologians to support the forces of the "law of the land" because of what the Supreme Court had discovered about the inhumanity of segregation—the justices in their wisdom changing their minds eighty years after they had last looked into the matter. Others warned that Christians had another authority for obedience to brotherhood which demanded precedence over any appeals to law and order. Nevertheless, as recently as three or four years ago many of our Christian leaders demanded the full weight of federal power to "end" racism, meaning the redneck racism of the Old Confederacy. Now we find that those who are almost hysterical about the Johnson - Nixon - Humphrey - Daley - Agnew - Reagan - Wallace - Muskie "law and order" nexus, and who plead for restraint and de-escalation in Vietnam and for moderation in the enforcement of law and order in the cities, are the same voices who in previous years were demanding that we preach support for the law of the land and pray that Congress and the President initiate new ones.

We do not have to say "we told you so," because as witness there is the 1968 Democratic convention inside Fortress Chicago; there is the work of the Chicago police department, functioning under Hon. Richard J. Daley, Mayor; there is the exploitation of fear in the appeal of all candidates for "law and order"; there are the ghettos, north and south, urban and suburban and rural, black and white.

But we did what we were told to do when we returned to the South a decade or so ago. We tried the route of electioneering and party activism. We leaped into the movement for the election of "better" men (especially of our own omnipresent concerned Christian laymen) on the national, state, and local levels. We attended the conventions of both parties in courthouses, in the prescription rooms of drugstores and in hotel suites. We registered to vote, and we preached about Christian citizenship and responsibility and took carloads to the polls. (And some were beaten unmercifully by other Christian citizens for their exercise of Christian citizenship.) But where has it taken us? Where has it taken us, and them? In part, it has taken us to the ethics professors who learned their theological lessons better than we did, who retain their objective passion to be "relevant," and who tell us that our policy in Vietnam is more Christian than our policy in World War II because of our restraint, for this time we are not demanding unconditional surrender! (Apparently, it is Christian realism to kill *some* babies and old people and young men, but it is not Christian realism to kill *all* babies and old people and young men.) It has brought us to the ethics professors, saying and writing wisely and seriously that, historically, the witness of America's statesmen (Rusk, McNamara, Ball, Kennan, Freeman) will prove more Christian than the witness of the Berrigans and Groppi. It has brought us, on the same premises, to organizations of Christian concern coalescing around selective wars, selective conscientious objection, and various theories about the draft as exercises in Christian realism. ("We disagree with the *tactics* of the Administration," or, "American *interest* is not involved," or, "We are not *pacifists*. God forbid! We supported the Kennedys in Cuba and Vietnam," etc.) It has brought high-ranking religious officials to address national denominational gatherings on the efficiency and the weakness of our ICBM system. (From expertise in banking and psychology is such a short journey to expertise in military strategy!) It has brought most religious editors and seminary deans and associate deans worthy of their expense accounts to comment with the authority, seriousness and unction of the modern Christian realist on every ripple and plop in the muck and mire of what Caesar says are domestic and international crises, to lecture expertly on economics and urban and suburban chaos, to muse about "the celebration of the arts and mass media," and to warn about the goings-on in Communist China.

Were we poorly advised? Or did we misunderstand? To repeat: it seems to us that we were brought by all this to an acceptance of Caesar's judgment about what is good and bad, right and wrong, just and unjust, critical and insignificant, lawful and likely to cause chaos. And this is the Baalism, the totalitarian quality of modern politics which we Christians have not only endured but encouraged. It seems to us that, in permitting ourselves to be brought here, we have rejected the one vocation we Christians have in and to the world, and that we have, in the name of realism and relevance, accepted willy-nilly the world's inhumanity to man as normal, and the politics of Caesar as Lord and Savior. By doing so, we have denied our birthright as Christ's sons and brothers, whose *only* task as his sons and brothers is to witness to what the risen Lord has already done for men: he made each of us a brother to the other, so that there is no need to kill if his skin is different or his politics repugnant. So also undoubtedly are our politics, and all politics, but for us it is no longer a matter of life and death.

The theologians were right when they told us that the proper reading was "God so loved *the world*," not "God so loved *the Church*." And we know they were right when they taught us that we ought to go *into the world* because that was what our Lord did. But what we are asking is whether or not there is any of *that* world in election politics, in political conventions, and in everything that necessarily precedes election politics and political conventions. We are not asking whether our Lord would have stayed out of political conventions and electioneering because of the deceit and compromise and chicanery that are properly a part of electoral politics: after all, he died for us, who are filled with deceit and compromise and chicanery (cf. Rom. 5, 8). Moreover, an Ed King in 1964 as chairman of the Mississippi Freedom Democratic Party is one thing; clergy delegates for Humphrey, McCarthy, Nixon, Rockefeller or Wallace are something else. Were there not tens of thousands ready to accept gladly, greedily, the posts held by the clergy-delegates who went to Chicago and Miami in 1968, just as there was not one who stood with Ed King *in* Mississippi (something quite different from standing with him in Atlantic City) in 1964?

We are asking whether the muck and mire in which we were told to immerse ourselves can be found anywhere in electioneering and political conventions. We are asking whether, in the end, it is not ridiculous for Christians to exhaust their witness to Christ in pathetic efforts to inject morality and high-mindedness into politics by "being there," up to their steeples. We are asking whether political conventions and the whole affair that is today called the political process is nothing but a façade, an illusion, a diversion, a temptation to keep us away from where, in muck and mire, most of us human beings play out our lives. We are asking whether true human existence is to be found in electioneering, or whether the world of election politics is today the place where we spend our energies after the politicians and political experts have jammed scales over our eyes so that we cannot see what we ought to see, so that we cannot note what is happening in the streets—for example, on both ends of the billy-clubs.

In a word, we are convinced that in our day the world of politics is in large part the world of illusions. We are convinced that if we Christians persist in our frantic desire to be relevant to politics, we shall end up as what we are in fact now: court prophets and priests of Baal. Is not our main function *as Christians* today a sanctification of political enterprises and adventures that were firmly contradicted by Christ and Scripture?

Render unto Caesar the things that are Caesar's. What we must reject is the effort of Caesar (the political order) to assert himself as the only authority on where the muck and mire of human existence are, to tell us that the only salvation for human existence is to be found in politics—as Caesar determines politics. And we must reject the Church's leading us into this service of Baal. We must reject Caesar's illusion that politics is the messiah for the human condition as well as the Church's sanction of this illusion. We must reject Caesar's seduction that politics is the only reality, and his claim that such a reality can best be served by Christians who are participating up to their gills in politics, contributing ethics and high-mindedness to political decisions. We must reject the Church's attempt to sanctify anything Caesar does by asking us to be priests of Baal so that we can be prophets of Christ. Baalism is the confession that God, the God of Abraham, Isaac, Jacob and Jesus Christ, is dead. And this Baalism of the contemporary Church is why Christian opposition to the horrors of Vietnam and the violence of the forces of law and order in our streets and backroads is ineffective as well as ambiguous. "What is cheaply given can be cheaply had." Who can take seriously Church pronouncements on anything today? Some would say that we simply do not know what would happen in political affairs if the Church did not try to bring morality to bear on the decision-making processes. We ask what, after all, did any clergy-delegate do or say at Miami or Chicago that was not done and said with more effectiveness, dignity and poise by the garden-variety delegate from Wisconsin, Nevada, Utah or Kansas.

We must reject the Church's—and Caesar's—insistence that only if Christians are concerned from moment to moment and from crisis to crisis will their work in the muck and mire of human existence be relevant and a true witness to Christ's victories. Has not that demand of the Church led us to Baal? What has Caesar to tell us about Christ's victory? We must reject the notion that the only words to the world the Christian has to offer are the cries in electioneering, petitions to the bureaucracy, and the participation up to the gills in political conventions. This merely sanctions all the ambiguities and idolatries of 20th-century political messianism, and renders nothing but folly to Caesar. What kind of service is it to politics to share the very illusions of messianism which have brought the world of the 20th century from two global wars—in an effort to restore peace—to the shadow of hydrogen apocalypse and world starvation—in the effort to save us from communism and preserve freedom? How do we walk with our Lord into the world if we do not follow him into the world but rather follow the very political messianism of Caesar which Christians, above all, are commanded to reject in obedience to the Lord, for the sake of Christ and the brothers?

The truth is that nothing happened in Chicago, Miami or Montgomery. The truth is that nothing happened on November 5, 1968, or will happen on November 3, 1970, etc. So let the Christian act as if nothing happened, behave as if nothing happened. That would mean, at least, living the sign of Jonah and not the sign of the swastika or donkey or elephant or eagle or hammer and sickle or Star of David. That would mean that the

Christian could render the *only* service he can make as a Christian to Caesar, to politics, the *only* vocation which would take him (with no advice from Caesar) into the muck and mire of human existence which our Lord guides with care and love. When, after all, did Jesus "act as if something were happening" in the political order that required him to immerse himself in it up to his gills? To live the sign of Jonah is to reject the temptation of Baal. To assert, in the muck and mire, by what we do and whom we visit, that Christ arose is to render more service than a convention's worth of clergy-delegates plunging heartily and with a briefcase full of analyses into political electioneering.

Is there any specific lesson to be learned from all this? Weep not! And weep!

Weep not for those who have "dropped out" of political participation, who are convinced that it can only get more idolatrous than it is now, and who believe that that dropping out may be the only realistic way of moving back in. After all, to refuse to drop out, to stay in, is in effect to stay in under the domination of Nixon and Daley, Humphrey, Wallace, Agnew and all the rest. That is one of the chief reasons our political priests and experts regularly preach that American democracy is identical with the two-party system. The Founding Fathers didn't think so. That is the real reason the American political system is paranoid today about both Wallace's candidacy and the youth who have decided to try to move politics into the street and away from the voting booths and law courts. It is not Wallace's racism or youth's radicalism that is offensive. It *is* their refusal to play out their frustration, anger, and powerlessness within the two-party consensus which has been for decades two-party in name only, not in reality or performance. Weep not for those who drop out.

But weep for those, especially Christians, who bit frantically and desperately, hook, line, sinker and fishpole, at the bait that the Christian—especially now as never before—must participate in the political processes to bring moral dimensions to the great issues, to the decision-makers. Weep for those. For the real decisions of 1968 in Chicago and Miami, in Washington and Detroit, were made in the streets, on both ends of the billy-clubs, and in the offices of the city bureaucrats and technicians, with the aid and support of the FBI, Secret Service, Pentagon, and concerned citizens. There was no lack of emotion and sentimentality, but there was only political illusion in the shouting and singing led by Mayor Daley and Theodore Bikel of "God Bless America!" and "The Battle Hymn of the Republic." There was only political illusion—no realism, political, Christian or otherwise—in the cheering and pseudo-TV-excitement about what happened or didn't happen on the Vietnam plank, or on the unit rule, or on speculations about a subordinate clause in the nominee's acceptance speech, or in the tears for a martyred leader. Weep for those who stayed in.

Is there any specific lesson to be learned? How about this? Some of our brothers are now pleading with Caesar to deny the clergy the temptation of privileged status regarding military conscription. We have a more simple—and, we feel, more relevant—formula for those who would deny themselves, one that does not require the interest or even the approval of Caesar— at least not at the present time. Let all Christian ministers, priests, theologians, bureaucrats and full-time Christian laymen deny themselves the temptation of Baalism, the temptation of political activism and participation. More specifically, let all ministers, priests, bureaucrats, theologians and full-time Christian laymen renounce, in a formal ceremony of the Church, their "right" to vote. Then we might learn something from them about living the sign of Jonah. God knows, there would be no political loss, for what have we contributed to the ethical thrusts that was not more competently and elegantly contributed by the delegates from Wisconsin, Nevada, Utah or Kansas?

What concerns us now is that we Christians are rendering to Caesar the things that are God's. And that is the politics of Baal, not the sign of Jonah.

What concerns us now is the Christian's complicity in setting the course irrevocably toward the technological police state, the Christian's effort to hand over the world to *politics*. And that is not the sign of Jonah but the politics of Baal.

XII
Our Grade Is "F"

From the Nina, the Pinta and the Santa Maria to the Mekong Delta, failure is a word never to be tolerated in American life. Throughout our history, we have always done whatever was necessary for success, even if we had to change what the word meant (as, yesterday, in the wars against the Indians, and, today, in Vietnam). Yet if one takes even a casual look at the American scene today, there is no cause to celebrate our successes. Instead, we are failing, and there is despair in the land. We are failing as a people, as a political entity, as a Christian community and as individual Christians.

Take the racial question. Writers, reporters, social scientists, experts on human relations, preachers, rabbis and priests who moved into the big and hopeful arena of integrating American culture ten or twenty years ago are now slowly and sadly turning to more promising fields of interest and service—observing or talking about the Sunday afternoon drag strip, farming, the local pool hall, crafts, breeding dogs, etc.

Ten years ago it was different. While Southern legislators and reactionary newspaper editors were screaming *"Never!"* we liberals were exuding optimism with our foundation grant and a well-written and organized table of procedure. The enemy stood as a clear target. The issues were clear-cut. To be sure there were not a lot of us, but the task was an obvious one. Get the nine black children into school. Get Governor Faubus to withdraw his troops. Get the federal troops here. Get the public schools open. All those things were accomplished, and some of us were a part of it. Ten years later things are not really better in America where the problem of race is concerned. They are worse. And in the name of progress—public housing, urban renewal, and model cities—a program of resegregation has begun. The target does not stand so clear today.

Ten years ago a handful of us in the occupied city of Little Rock, Arkansas, walked to school the first day with the nine black children. We felt fresh and clean inside. But today we would hesitate to take that same walk, not for fear of a governor's National Guard, but for fear of meeting the jeers of "Honky, go home!"

No longer can we identify the enemy so easily. No longer can we isolate the issues. We are denied issues. No longer do we battle against flesh and blood, but against principalities and powers, spiritual wickedness in high places. There is despair in the land. There is failure in the land.

What happened? Perhaps we started too late. Perhaps we chose the wrong enemy in the first place. Or perhaps, like Israel, our sins do not permit us to turn to God (Hos. 5, 4); perhaps we could not turn from our wicked ways if we wanted to. There comes a time when even repentance is impossible and only judgment remains. Perhaps those we sought to help had already seen too much of us. Perhaps they alone knew who we really were. They had seen what Vincent Harding reminds us of: the burning of the Indians by our Puritan fathers while they gave thanks to God. They had seen the concentration camps we created for those first families. They had seen our rape of Mexico, the crushing of the Cuban rebellion in 1898 and the destruction of the Philippine revolution in the years that followed. They had watched our constant domination of the Latin nations. They heard the accusation by one of their leaders that World War I was primarily the jealous and avaricious struggle for the larger share in exploiting the dark races. They watched us in World War II as we began a holy war but ended in setting loose the most monstrous of all weapons, so monstrous that, in 25 years, only we have used it.

They see us now in Vietnam.

Is it any wonder that we are charged now with genocide? And let us be honest enough to examine that charge as it is used by Stokely Carmichael, Rap Brown and others. When these men use it, they don't mean simply that America would choose to exterminate physically all people of color, though there is mounting evidence that this is precisely what we will do if we have to.

Let us remember that the charge was first made at the time when the most rapid strides were being taken toward integration, when civil rights legislation was being passed, when presidents and southern mayors were joining hands and singing "We Shall Overcome." Why do you suppose they talk about genocide? Because it began to be evident to black men what we meant by integration. Black men began to see what Markus Barth had pointed out to us five years ago, that while white, good, liberal Americans were open to the social needs, necessities and opportunities of the present hour, there was a condition to it. They began to see that we were willing, yes, even eager, to receive blacks into *our* schools, *our* neighborhoods, *our* jobs, *our* clubs, perhaps *our* churches (sometimes), and even into our families and bedrooms. But they also saw that our understanding of the end of segregation was usually identified with that kind of acceptance which presupposes, among other things, that there are two cultures, two races, two types of men, a hierarchy of creation. "Integration" came to mean the active pursual of a course allowing the two races to encounter each other in such a way that the white partner could forgive his black brother for being black and permit him to become an honorary white man. Nothing more was required of blacks other than that they learn their lessons: keep their yards clean, keep their voices down, wash themselves at least once a day, enjoy the treasures of higher culture, stabilize their courtship and marriage customs, just as the white man is alleged to have done. The beginning of genocide is not ovens and concentration camps. The beginning of genocide is the beginning of integration: the expectation of the majority that the minority will become like the majority.

What we tried to peddle was racial migration, and we failed

to sell it. We failed because it was a faulty commodity. It was no more than segregation turned inside out. And the first faint cry of black power scared us so badly that we quickly, immediately, distorted it to mean not what it originally did mean—namely, the development of political movements capable of securing just demands as other American minorities have done. We distorted black power to mean what white power has meant all these centuries—a ruthless ruling by the powerful of the powerless. Thus we stand as failures because we deserved to have failed.

We have failed on the racial front in the second place because *every* institution of our culture has found a way out of meeting the crisis. The sin of the responsible institutions of culture is not that they have lied, but that they have carefully and cunningly manipulated the truth—each with its own shibboleth, each with its own idol. The god of the racist is racial supremacy. But we were smart enough and good enough to isolate that. Grant him his premise, and you cannot beat him. We rightly identified his grave sin as idolatry. But we did not realize that in the process we were creating our own idol and idols. One idol after another was brought into play which in effect excused us of any real responsibility.

American industry today argues for and hides behind the false god of "merit employment." Let's give them a test. Those who make the highest score will get the job. Guess who gets the job? The tests are written by people who for the most part know about pheasant-under-glass. If you ask some ghetto child about pheasant-under-glass, he makes zero. But ask him about the breeding habits of cockroaches or how a rat can crawl up an iron crib and gnaw the toes and fingers off his baby sister, and he will make a good grade while the middle-class applicant will make zero. Thus we have the modern idol of merit employment.

Another example is the American press with its idol of objectivity. The importance of fair and impartial coverage of the news is valid. But it is not enough in this day of national

Our Grade Is "F"

peril simply to react to, report and shoot pictures of the various crises. In wartime, the press is always filled with pages of patriotic slogans designed to support the leadership in an emergency. The press does not hesitate to propagandize for other good causes—the UGF, Boy Scouts, National Science Week. But when it comes to the human situation of *race*, though there are notable exceptions, the press is piously faithful to the cult of objectivity and sends this great tragedy back to the racist, white and black, to be solved.

Another example is the Church in America with its concern for peace and harmony within the fellowship—a valid concept, no doubt, until we consider that the man whom many of us call "Lord" used the Church primarily as a place to raise hell.

Another example is "education." The American colleges and universities (Christian and otherwise) have carefully avoided any involvement in the racial crisis by worshiping at the shrine of academic excellence. The president of a great Southern university remarked to us a few years ago, once it had been decided, after all that time, to admit 5 or 6 *qualified black students* and we had been summoned by someone other than the president to serve as "consultants" to the situation: "We don't contemplate any problem here because there won't be many to measure up to our high standards." He spoke the truth. In this way higher education washes its hands pure in the *Pilate* basin of academic excellence and sends the problem back to the racist, black and white. But it is doubtful that the shibboleth of academic standards is ultimately any more sacred to God than the hue and cry of racial intermarriage—the shibboleth of the deep South racist—is sacred to God. Both, no doubt, contain an element of some sort of "truth": both are worshiping false gods.

The failure of education requires a closer look at dimensions that include, but go beyond, the racial one. An important reason why the racial catastrophe is deep and probably irreversible is what America now means by and does with "education." Education's failure, together with the perversion of education which came about in the process of failing in the racial crisis, is probably the most monumental calamity to befall an institution of American culture in the twentieth century. The refusal "to bus" in order to achieve some degree of balance leading toward an effective primary and secondary educational process, and the failure of higher education to seek out in order to serve the victims of this process, are simply the two most obvious manifestations of the same calamity.

We are concerned here, however, with the failure of education that falls as an especially acute judgment on the Christian in America. The New Testament proclaims the Good News that religion—that sickness which binds man to himself and to his idols and images—is conquered by the resurrection. What concerns us is the fact that "education" has become a religion in the American democracy (and to the Church) more sacred than democracy itself (and Christ). The New Testament makes it clear that "education" is not "evangelism." What concerns us is the fact that the gamut of activities that goes by the name "education"—that activity which was to be the sure and certain guarantee that the American people would become free and continue to live in freedom and democracy—along with and urgently supported by the political order, is preparing our minds and souls for the technological concentration camp.

We are concerned about more than a virtue that has become a vice, a thesis that has become an antithesis, a tragedy that is more than intellectual because it involves the souls of the humanists and the birthright of Christians. We are convinced, for example, that the gut decisions that Christians will face in the next years and decades will not primarily concern military service (it is more efficient to have a voluntary, professional army) but rather service to the idol of American "education." We believe that Christians will soon be forced to make decisions about whether to permit their children to attend institutions (from kindergarten upward, Christian and secular), spawned by educational systems and bureaucracies that are already hopelessly closed, totalitarian and beyond hope of internal or external renewal, and whose efforts produce a generation of youth either cynical because of the manifest hypocrisy or brainwashed as to value and meaning in life. And Christians must make those decisions—like all decisions made as Christians—in the light of the fact that it is the Good News, and not "education," which liberates captives from the dungeons of idolatry.

Christians are more confused than anyone today about what "education" *is*. Or perhaps most Christians are not confused, but rather naively assume that they know what education *is*—and that, today, is to be far, far worse off than to be confused. But the real charge that must be leveled against Christians is that it was not us, but the plethora of revolts by blacks, youth, police, Indians, etc., which challenged all our easy, liberal assumptions about what "education" *is*. Is education, for example, the objective transmission of information, data, facts and skills about sundry subjects, liberating the recipient from ignorance about certain information, data, facts, skills—so that choices may be made on the basis of "reason," and every choice made by those receiving this information, data, etc., is thereby "rational"? Perhaps so. But who decides what information, data, facts and skills will be transmitted, and by whom, and why may we trust one person's objectivity and reject another's as subjective and emotional?

Or is education the appreciation of cultural, especially Western, traditions, enabling one to better understand the world and the time in which we live? Perhaps so. But who decides how to present what about which tradition? For example, shall we agonize and assign term papers about the "meaning" of the Protestant Reformation and the Age of Reason, and thus ignore the "meaning" of the introduction of the traffic in black lives from Africa to the "new" world by white Christian ladies and gentlemen? Shall we chart the battle of New Orleans and the Bloody Angle, and thus deny Christian genocide against the original inhabitants of what we now call North and Central and South America? Shall we memorize Talcott Parson's theory of social action and overlook J. Edgar Hoover's?

Some believe that education is the great equalizer in American democracy. Accessible to all regardless of race, creed and color, it is the one sure vehicle which permits a son or daughter of a black mother and white father to attend public schools anywhere without prejudice or impediment, secure admission into the crack universities or Christian liberal arts colleges, and become Abraham Lincoln, Richard Nixon, Betty Furness, Jonas Salk or Neil Armstrong. The fact is that tax-supported education (and *all* education, some Baptists and others to the contrary notwithstanding, *is* tax-supported) aids upper- and middle-income children far more than it supports these lower-income folk. Indeed, these folk—because of who they are and what America has done to them and where they live—are the victims of the very educational system which their own tax dollars support in a higher proportion than do upper- and middle-income families. This fact we hereby commend to the earnest consideration of trustees in the small Christian college who are concerned about the separation of Church and State, government support, etc.—not that they accept government support, but that they recognize an indebtedness to those who support *them*. And what about the black man's blackness, the red man's redness, etc., in education today? It is a "problem" which requires a "solution": those who are different because of skin color or "cultural deprivation" are made into "white"—in public institutions under the rubric of democracy, in Christian institutions under the rubric of brotherhood.

Some hold to a robust American pragmatism: we know what education is when we see what it does. On that score, also, we question an easy assurance. Education in the United States has studied war and the decision-making and political processes and power politics so thoroughly since World War II that a class of American mandarins has been created by our graduate schools. But this educational process, itself an object of critical professional inquiry only very recently—that is, after the barn had burned with the horses inside—has offered no alternative to the cold war, to worldwide insurrections of race and poverty, to an understanding of the Middle Eastern crises that are surely wrenching Hitler's victims there into his own violent image and that are not without racial touches. As for

Vietnam, it is the crown jewel of those scientists of human affairs (especially political affairs) who reject even the moral judgments of humanity as weak and subjective intrusions into the world of political realism.

Education today might well be judged by what it does. And what we see it doing is adjusting the student to "the system" which is everywhere. In other words, it is dehumanizing the student rather than liberating him. Education should work toward an adjustment of "the system" which is to serve humanity. But because education today is an adjustment of the student to the system, the great people and the great literature and the great music and the great art since World War II have not been the work of those who are a part of the educational institutions in America. How could they be? And because this is so, our educational institutions are prisoners of the manifold fruits of a technology which the helpless and impoverished of the world and our land know only too well, from Hiroshima to Hanoi, from Canton in Mississippi to Ocean Hill-Brownsville in New York. And because this is so, education, wherever it might take place, must begin as a process of *dis*-adjustment to "the system." And *that*, brothers and sisters, is about all we know of what "education" *is* today.

Where are the Christian colleges in all of this? Where they have always been, led by Caesar and his educational institutions and bureaucracies, except that, in most cases, we were early to segregate racially, in order to be relevant to our people, and late to desegregate because we had to preserve "unity"; and because of the strength of our conviction that our intentions are of the highest and purest quality, we are the last to understand that integration is, in fact, another way to control "them."

Whom does the Christian college serve? Whom do Caesar's colleges serve? The same people, and precious few others. Certainly not the victims of Caesar's educational Gestapos, for these are "high risk." And no one (Caesar's servants or Christ's) gives any thought to how high the risk *any* student runs by devoting four irretrievable years of his life to the sickness of present-day educational establishments. Certainly there is little enthusiasm in the Christian colleges today to resurrect those of whom Jonathan Kozol speaks in *Death at an Early Age*. For which among the present-day colleges has been more anxious about the dodges and deceits called "quality education" and "academic excellence" than the Christian liberal arts college? Which among them has been more anxious about accreditation than the Christian liberal arts college, even though it meant a service to Caesar and a denial of the service to Christ? Which among the educational institutions has competed more enthusiastically and energetically with Caesar for high-quality students (so as not "to scrape the bottom of the barrel"), and for basketball players, faculty, coaches, science centers and athletic stadiums, than the Christian liberal arts college? Which among the colleges has ignored more effectively than the Christian liberal arts college the stranger lying bloody in the ditch (cf. Lk. 10, 29ff.), the victim of the very educational system which now denies him?

Whom does the Christian liberal arts college serve when it echoes Caesar's concerns about "qualifications," academic standards, SAT and CEEB and GRE scores? In whose service is the Christian liberal arts college when it fails to strike head on the very concept of "qualification," especially qualifications defined by the educational brigands who consigned the victim, bruised, naked and half-dead, into the sewers of American society, dug in part by the educational brigands themselves? Whom does the Christian liberal arts college serve when it does not lead an onslaught against the totalitarianism of accrediting agencies? Where is the Christian liberal arts college which has compassion even on her own victims as well as Caesar's by pouring on oil (and, yes, wine) and paying the bill, not in reparations but as a neighbor.

What we are asking is: Where in the Christian college is the white youngster we call a "Kluxer" because he doesn't know which side of the plate the salad fork goes on and spends a lot of time talking about sex and automobiles? Where in the Christian college is the black whom we call "culturally de-

Our Grade Is "F" 139

prived" and thus ineligible for admission to higher education because he has been deprived (or spared) *our* culture and belches or crepitates in public?

(Let none think, however, that our questions have already been given answers by the Bob Jones university types. We have another set of questions for them, centering around their own capitulation to the techniques of contemporary totalitarianism. The fact is that a few, but not many, of our readers are inheritors of the Bob Jones traditions. A great many of us are debtors to the Christian liberal arts college.)

Our Christian colleges speak for mammon, not God. There is precious little evidence that they—that is, their trustees or administrators or faculties or alumni or students—desire the humility to do otherwise than be an agent of mammon. Against what we are saying it may be argued that the Christian liberal arts college is serving Christians—or at least the progeny of Christians—in America. But when was the principal service to Christ ever the rendering of service to ourselves (cf. Lk. 10, 29ff)? In our Christian colleges we are in fact serving ourselves and not Christ, in the middle- and upper-income orientation of our curriculum and faculty and administration and trustees. Our distaste for the victims of our economics is never more evident than in our loud shouts about how many more "Negroes," how many "high-risk" students we admitted than last year, how many more than the state university, how many more than the Ivy League colleges. If we were in the least bit serious about black and high-risk students, why would we have to say anything about *them?* Why not, like the man in Luke 10, 29ff., *be* compassionate by binding up wounds and paying the bills and leaving, *incognito?*

Christian colleges, unlike the medieval universities we like to deplore so much because of their authoritarianism, are contemptuous toward their environments—human and natural—which are exploited rather than served. Christian colleges have constructed buildings and obtained operational capital from a rape of the land and from the sweat and backs of Indians, blacks, rednecks, hillbillies, Kluxers, Chicanos, peckerwoods, etc. The Christian colleges then use them as service or maintainence lackeys, while their pathetic little culture-starved MA's and Ph.D's ridicule and scoff them and their music and dress and antics and drinking and fighting and sex life and prose and vocabulary and support of George Wallace, and tell lies about them (and thereby about middle- and- upper-income Americans and Christians) in their "required" courses.

Our Christian colleges serve themselves and not Christ when they explain in the most pained tones that they have only so "many" resources and that these must be allocated on the basis of priorities. And what and who are the priorities? Ourselves. Middle- and upper-income Christian Americans. And these are the priorities set by Caesar, not by Christ. They are, the Christian colleges insist, committed to "quality education." Spelled out, this means that our Christian colleges will continue their commitment to the very same cycle of events which put and keeps the victims of the educational system, bloodied and bruised and half-dead, in the sewer of American society. And because he smells badly since he has been there so long, the Christian liberal arts college covers the victim not with oil and wine and compassion, but with surveys, institutional self-studies, statements of purpose and massive foundation requests (that were rejected). An allocation of resources based on commitments to "quality education" is simply the educator's "white" lie that a commitment to the victims of the educational system in America is a compromise of "quality education." And this is quite simply the racism of white intransigence, which feeds on a conviction of superiority that crucified Christ and recrucifies him anew.

Christ have mercy on us! What is the *quality* of "quality education" that rejects Christ's own dying for *all* men? Where is the quality in what our Christian colleges have taught about what Christian white people have done in wars and slavery to the people of color the world over, and what we have done in our own peculiar wars against each other? Where is the *excellence* that judges it "excellent" to allocate resources to support and preserve the very institutions and ways of life that raped a people and a land and imported the children of God as draft animals, that digs new sewers in which to throw the new victims created by the new systems and methods and techniques of the American way of life?

Where is the service to Christ in that myriad of Christian liberal arts colleges whose only boast over the hated (because of the larger budget) state university is the lower student-teacher ratio (which never really works out to smaller classes in a meaningful way), easy access to the teachers, and the absence of student-faculty radicalism and hippie types? There is *no* service to Christ in all this, for the simple reason that there is no essential difference between what is happening on the campus of the Christian liberal arts college and that of the large state university. Using the same formulas, both compete in recruiting the same students, for the same curriculum, taught by instructors indoctrinated by the same prejudices of the same professors in the same graduate and professional schools—except that instructors at the state universities were, for the most part, better all-round students, have stronger and more realistic and relevant views of today's society, and (unbelievable as it might seem) are on the whole better classroom teachers. (What is the sense in bragging about smaller classes if the students are presided over by imperialistic old maids, male and female?)

So there it is: Students sharing the same presuppositions because they must have them to finish high school and be "admitted" to college; faculty sharing the same ones because they have to get a "degree" and an "appointment" and tenure, promotions and sabbaticals; administrators sharing them because they have to allocate resources according to the priorities set by society and by Caesar's universities, and by trustees drawn from the specialists in making and raising money in the American system. There they are: the Christian college and the state university, together and indistinguishable, not under the cross but under the great yum-yum tree of academic excellence and quality education. There are no distinctions between "education" and "evangelism" wrought on the cross, but rather the "cross" in the "classroom" and not on *Golgotha*—evangelism in the service and at the beck and call of education-as-adjustment to the system which is all around us.

But why should we emphasize failures only? Why not, for

a change, speak of successes? Because there are no successes. Because insofar as the Christian college is concerned, there will be no successes, absolutely not one, unless and until the nature and the depth of the failure are seen and accepted. And this lies not in our hands, but in God's. We are under his judgment.

It is clear that there will be no successes until the Christian college grasps the difference between teaching and evangelism as seen in the New Testament. Then it will cease evangelizing education by the cheap trick of trying to put "Christ in the classroom." Look for success, then, not in Christian colleges because they call themselves Christian. Look for success in a student here, a "call to discipleship" yonder, an insight there from a teacher which makes it impossible to "study" war or racism or the New Testament and come away the same person, impossible to study the political processes and sell one's soul to them, impossible to study physics or chemistry and not dedicate one's career to opposing their enslavement to the horrors of 20th-century technological inhumanity, impossible to study money and banking and come away lighthearted at what our economics have done to those who originally had property rights to the land which supports us so richly, and to those whom we purchased as chattel and continue to treat as such. Look for success not where "Christ," but a socratic Christian, is in the classroom—that is, a teacher who will put *everything* under question and accept *nothing* at face value (especially himself and his discipline), not for the hell of it or because he is possessed of a demon, but because the cross and the resurrection put *everything* under question. Yesterday, today, forever. *Everything.*

Look for success in those places, for not under any circumstance is it essential that this kind of success occur only on the campus or in the classroom of the Christian liberal arts college. *That is the point.*

And that is why we speak of failure.

We wish, finally, to talk about another failure, the failure of the Church and society to distinguish between the so-called black problem and the problem of the poor whites. Our nation has refused to see this distinction, we suspect, partly because of our accumulated guilt and partly because we assumed that the problem of race offered more promise of solution. We white liberals romanticized the racial problem and sought to identify with the civil rights movement either by ignoring the poor white or by seeing movements, which manifest themselves most often in such groups as the Ku Klux Klan, as a police problem, pure and simple.

A few years ago the Columbia Broadcasting System did a documentary film called "The Ku Klux Klan: An Invisible Empire." It showed the horror of such things as the murder of Goodman, Chaney and Schwerner in Mississippi, the castration of Judge Aaron in Alabama, and the murder of four Sunday school children in Birmingham. Who would deny that they were dreadful crimes? But, as always, there were many important things which were not put before the audience, most important being the conditions which produced these people. The same thing produced them that produces—and is producing and will produce—more violence in the black ghetto. These same things are producing the white ghettos and will produce the violence, the rioting and all the rest.

The film did not tell about a friend of ours who is a leader in the Ku Klux Klan. It did not tell about how his father left him when he was six years old or how his mother then went to work in a textile sweat shop, where for 37 years her job was to sew the seam down the right leg of overalls. The *outside* right leg, for 37 years—never the inside of the right leg, never the left leg; her job for 37 years was to make the seam down the right side of the overalls, and that was for 40 cents an hour, and generally for not more than 2 days a week. They did not tell us about how this boy ran away, joined the Army at 14, was jumping out of airplanes as a paratrooper when he was 16, and was leading a platoon when he was 18. The film didn't tell how for 17 years he learned the fine arts of torture, interrogation and guerrilla warfare.

The film said that only the Ku Klux Klan has a record of violence as an organization. What of the textile industry sweat shops? What of the American Legion? (What of us—and how much do you pay your maid or your maintenance personnel? How many hungry children are there in your town tonight?)

The film did not tell us that the same social forces producing the Klan's violence produced the violence of Watts, Rochester, Harlem, Cleveland, Chicago, Dayton, Tampa, Houston, Atlanta, Baton Rouge and Nashville. The Klansmen are of the same stuff, victims of the same social isolation, deprivation, economic conditions, rejections, underemployment and unemployment, broken homes, working mothers, ignorance, poor schools, no hospitals, bad diets, and all the rest. Does one have to wonder why the film did not tell us?

The invisible empire? Yes, there is an invisible empire in America, but it is not the Ku Klux Klan.

There is a film of an invisible empire which needs to be made. It should be of the evil and cynical white aristocracy, the few, not in the South but in America, who profited from the sale of human flesh. It should include those who tried to do something about their plight in the Populist movement and the Farmers' Alliance in the 1890's. It should report how the poor, ignorant rednecks were told that if they persisted in their egalitarian activities, their daughters would be ravished *en masse* by blacks. Then the camera should be turned slightly to the northeast, to the little city of Springfield, Massachusetts, where can be found what is said to be the richest street in the world, built not with Yankee ingenuity, but with the sale of rum and slaves. Let there be a few frames for a beautiful upper-class church edifice there, and for its pastor who several years ago said at a very fashionable luncheon that his most annoying problem was one usher who insisted on walking down the aisle in the offering procession in a gray flannel suit instead of the traditional morning cutaway which the other five ushers wore. Let that portion of the film conclude with this same pastor asking of a fellow clergyman from the South in all seriousness, "Do you think the churches of the South will ever wake up and do something about this race problem?"

And if it is to be a film on the invisible empire, then let the electronic devices turn to the political processes in this country, from the capitol dome to the courts, the police stations, the banks, and the savings and loan companies. They are all run not by Kluxers, but by people of the middle and upper incomes, all of them respectable and responsible citizens. And then do not forget again the universities (Christian and otherwise) which —at best, insofar as blacks and other minorities are concerned —recruit those whose cultures and manners are already white, and which, where poor whites are concerned, use their intellect and influence to convince this country's people that those who can't afford to go to or qualify for college should be the ones to go and fight this nation's wars, so that those who can afford to go to college can remain in the safety and security of the ivory towers. Finally, film those rejects of the intellectuals as they are taught to hate and kill and burn and interrogate and torture in the fine art of guerrilla warfare. Film them as they come back home and try to get an even break with the college educated. Watch them as they try to get back into "decent society." Document it with some words of President Johnson a few years ago when he pointed his long, bony finger at the millions in his television audience and said to the Klan, "Get out of the Klan and back into decent society while there is still time"—a remark which rings loudly of a police state. Watch the reject as he tries to go back into "decent society," and watch the door as it slams shut in his face. Where else can he go but to the Klan? Who else will have him? Who else wants a boy who was a big somebody in uniform but who is nobody's darling now? And yes, give some footage to the churches who have taught him racism in one way or another from the day he was born—all very decently, all very respectably, all for very good reasons—to preserve the harmony (that is, the wealth) of the institution.

Then let us talk about those who run this invisible empire— the ones who created the Klan, and Harlem, Watts, and Southside Chicago. We will show you an invisible empire that intervenes in an Asian civil war, an invisible empire which calculates exactly the amount of civil rights legislation that can be passed in this country without the white voting backlash becoming a reality, an invisible empire which deprives this country of an adequate health program and a guaranteed annual income so that no child in this rich land, be he Kluxer or Black Nationalist, must go hungry, uneducated, and uncared for medically.

We are not talking about hating the rich. We are simply saying that the invisible empire in this country is far more subtle, far more insidious, cunning and treacherous than a few hundred people gathered in a cow pasture around a burning cross. It has *always* been against the law to dynamite churches and burn houses and shoot housewives on public highways. Why then all the HUAC investigations of a group of folks in the deep South? Why indeed? Because what HUAC represents has always been pitted against Southern rednecks. Because we like to simplify problems. We like to find the Jonah and throw him overboard, assured that everything will then be all right.

In the beginning of our history we called ourselves the American "experiment." So did Abe Lincoln. We still do. It was a new and novel idea. As in any experiment, however, it is necessary from time to time to evaluate the data. Any scientist periodically will take a look at what he is doing, make changes, and start all over. Perhaps that time has now come in our history.

Whatever the reasons for our failure, however, let us turn briefly to the consequences. And the most glaring and obvious consequence, it seems to us, is that we are moving rapidly toward a contemporary police state. But we must be careful about that phrase. The images of an "American Hitler" or "Stalin" usually come to mind, with exiles, barbed-wire concentration camps, midnight knocks on the door, edicts suspending the Congress, judiciary and Constitution, the rounding up of potential enemies of the State, and government by the super-generals in the Pentagon and HEW technicians, presided over by the former Chief-of-Staff and the Vice President of the regime that was overthrown. But there is no need for that sort of thing. It is mainly a figment of the liberal's anomie, or the *Schadenfreude* of their money-raisers after they lose elections—not

Our Grade Is "F" 147

to George Wallace or General Edwin Walker, but to one equally as "liberal" as their own candidate.

We have argued for years that this is *not* the way it is going. The danger is not an American "Hitler," or even an American "Stalin" or "Mao." Such a one would fail for the same reason that Goliath failed against David. We are too cunning, too realistic, too educated, to permit the Goliath of an American Hitler to prevail over us. We would always have enough education to identify Goliath. We could always storm the concentration camps. We could always give our bodies to be burned as we chanted "Freedom! Freedom!"

The opportunity for that sort of martyrdom will be denied us in the technological concentration camp of our era and heritage. William Faulkner had a notion of it when he wrote about our white forefathers coming to these lands "not to escape from tyranny as they claimed and believed, but to establish one." *Ours.* Our tyranny. All quite fitting, proper, legal and democratic—and technological. For the concentration camps we are creating in this country are going up along the lines we have already suggested: A little rioting last summer. A little less this summer. Put it down quietly and quickly. Get better weapons—an armored personnel carrier and lots of gas. Establish better central communications. Work out pacts with the police, fire departments and National Guards of sister states. Use computers. A policeman is killed in Nashville or Los Angeles, and authorities say that Black Power is responsible. Raid their offices and their homes. So what if the courts under prodding from the ACLU say that it was "illegal"! Let them redo what has already been destroyed or burned. Let the judges come down and stop the next raid with their pieces of paper: we are Law, too. Pick up blacks with Afro cuts and say they looked like Eldridge (or Kathleen) Cleaver or Rap Brown or Stokely Carmichael. Then just pick up blacks, or Chicanos. A leader disappears in Chicago; another disappears in Waycross, Georgia—not to be heard from again, and nowhere for the family to go for help. But this is the exception, so that it will never be reported by Huntley-Brinkley or studied by the American Political Science Association, since there were not enough facts for generalization. People become distrustful. They look suspiciously at everyone in the dime store and supermarket and cocktail lounge: maybe he belongs to Black Power; maybe he works for the police or FBI. Any incident is quickly put down because American technology and foreign policy are spawning a nice and successful industry in newer gadgets for people-control. Try them out to see if they work. Only a few were killed. We can now spray ten square blocks with glue, sticking everyone together, or pour a sort of liquid banana peeling on the streets, or drop a plastic balloon from a helicopter—they can't burn and loot then! No riots now. Moreover, it would be a very amusing and educational sight, the knowledgeable but objective and impersonal Walter Cronkite giving TV explanations of the workings of these newest technological miracles: ten square blocks of people squirming and twisting and wiggling and falling, trying to get out. Very funny—unless you are an old woman, or a baby, or unless such an experience left a trauma on your soul that caused you to wake up screaming about it from a padded cell years hence. Of course, TV news cannot be expected to cover such individual matters. But there will be few killed; indeed, the number of fatalities will be liberally reduced if not wholly eliminated.

Riding south of the city of Chicago a couple of summers ago, we were shown by our host all the magnificent new housing developments, with mile after mile of high-rise apartments. "Look at that one," he explained enthusiastically. "The children never have to go outside! A school and a supermarket are inside there. A doctor is there. A hospital is there. A church. They *never* have to go outside!"

How in God's name can you riot there? You can control a half a million people with the turn of a master key, held by a democratically elected official. No killings. No riots. Everything goes merrily on its usual way. Law and order. We are in that concentration camp, and the mark of its efficiency is that we don't know we're in it, for how could anyone willingly and freely commit himself to a concentration camp? We only did what had to be done. But, after all, we made the decisions, for we voted in the progressives and supported their programs. We are members of—or at least vote for—one of the two parties which turn the switches and roll the dials and feed the computers. We studied the political processes in required college courses and learned about our world come-of-age from the religion teachers. We read *The Gospel According to Peanuts.* Thus we know we are where we are because of our own free, democratic choices. There are no concentration camps here, no barbed wire, no sadistic guards making us perform unspeakable acts, no camp administrators stretching tattooed human flesh over lampshade frames, no ovens stoked with human bodies, no numbers burned on our forearms, no Anne Frank and Dietrich Bonhoeffer and Heinrich Himmler and Joseph Goebbels. We are free because we did only what had to be done. And if we did it, are we not then free?

If that is what is coming, why go on? Why do we go on trying? Well, we don't go on trying. Trying is not what we must do. We go on not because of our ideals, but because of what God did for us in Christ. We go on because of that imperative of the verb which we have been speaking of throughout these pages: "Be reconciled!" *Katallagete!* Be what you are. Be what God's new creation in Christ has made you. We do not go on in the name of social action, for social action negates, turns away from, denies God's new creation in Christ.

We cannot make an order out of an ideal. However, we can participate in the order already made, not by us, but for us—for all of us—in Christ.

XIII
What Are We Going To Do Now?

Some young and old friends of ours, who have seen these chapters and said some polite things about them, often comment: "But you never make concrete suggestions for action. You always stop before you say what the Christian is supposed to *do!* All talk must lead to action. What are *we* going to do?"

Is this what *Katallagete,* being reconciled to God, is all about? "What are *we* going to do?" *Our* action?

We are so conditioned and trained by the power the *world* has over us that we believe that we, as Christians and as the Church, are *doing* "something" only when we do the same things everyone else does: send all the staff the budget will allow to scurry around every boondock and ghetto, dispensing weak tea and sympathy for the victims of the American way, so that the program can be written up as a budget request for next year; hold conferences which import articulate black radicals and articulate poor white militants for the sole purpose of leading us to cry out: "By God! We are guilty as hell! So how can we help you?" (the conferences seldom import the *in*articulate and *un*lovely victims because they remind us of who we are, and that they are the victims of who we are); sponsor voter registrations, petitions, rent strikes and protest marches against anything; involve the middle-class churchman up to his steeple in (liberal) politics; conduct seminars and consultations on "next steps" in race relations, war, disarmament, the draft and urban renewal; infiltrate the political structure as speech writers and research associates; launch projects which interview our victims in the ghettos to determine which among them qualifies for the charity of this particular member of Christ's body.

In any case, double the existing staff, create staff where there is none, hold at least two emergency conferences on every issue the world classifies as a "crisis," appoint members for an Afro-American studies program and call it a "curriculum enrichment committee," and, above all, do a survey.

This is what we Christians do and are expected to do, because this is the power of the "what are *we* going to do?" which the world holds over us. What we are asking is whether this sort of "what are *we* going to do?" has anything to do with the Christian—today! If someone questions the authority of this, we cite Jesus' account of who a neighbor *is* (Lk. 10, 29ff.) and his consistent refusal to become obsessed with Herod's influence, or with overthrowing Caesar—to say nothing of trying to inject "morality" into the nomination and election of a liberal President and Congress.

In the past few years, we have done our share of seminars, conferences, panels and "next step" consultations, urging the very same message. Toward the end of the question-and-answer period, someone usually shrieks: "Why, you're saying, 'Do nothing! Do *nothing!*'" And that is when we know we're coming through. That is when we say: "Brothers, just nail *that* down. Now you have the message. Do *nothing! Be* something!"

A friend of ours, Tom Merton, liked to remind us that "Bonhoeffer himself said it was an 'Anglo-Saxon failing' to imagine that the Church was supposed to have a ready answer for every social problem." Another friend of ours, John Howard Griffin, gave the best interpretation we know of what that good Trappist meant. "What can we, as Christians, do to help?" is the perennial question that the oppressor demands of his victim. "Before you do a damned thing," Tom would comment, "just *be* what you say you are, a Christian; then no one will have to tell you what to do. You'll know."

Do? *Nothing.* Be? What you are—*reconciled,* to God and man.
Katallagete!
Ad majorem Dei gloriam

www.ingramcontent.com/pod-product-compliance
Lightning Source LLC
Chambersburg PA
CBHW070907160426
43193CB00011B/1396

9 781592 449088